TRAEGER GRILL COOKBOOK:

100 Amazing Recipes for Beginners and Advanced Pitmasters, learn how to Smoke meat with specific instruction.

Steven Franklin

Table Of Contents

INTRODUCTION..8

TRAEGER WOOD PELLET GRILL...12

    HOW IT WORKS 13
    TRAEGER WOOD PELLET GRILL VS. CHARCOAL AND WOOD GRILLS 14
    PELLETS TO USE 14
    BENEFITS OF THE WOOD PELLET SMOKER-GRILL.......................... 15

WHAT YOU CAN COOK WITH YOUR TRAEGER 18

    COOKING TEMPERATURES, TIMES, AND DONENESS: 20

CLEANING AND MAINTENANCE 22

TIPS TO SUCCEED 24

GRILL BEEF RECIPES 28

    BEEF TENDERLOIN.. 29
    MUSTARD BEEF SHORT RIBS 30
    SWEET & SPICY BEEF BRISKET 31
    BRANDY BEEF TENDERLOIN.. 32
    BEEF RUMP ROAST 33
    HERBED PRIME RIB ROAST 34
    SPICY CHUCK ROAST.. 35

GRILL PORK RECIPES 36

    SMOKED AVOCADO PORK RIBS... 36
    SMOKED HONEY - GARLIC PORK CHOPS 37
    SMOKED PORK BURGERS.. 38
    SMOKED PORK CHOPS MARINATED WITH TARRAGON 39
    SMOKED PORK CUTLETS IN CITRUS-HERBS MARINADE 40
    SMOKED PORK CUTLETS WITH CARAWAY AND DILL 41
    SMOKED PORK LOIN IN SWEET-BEER MARINADE 42
    SMOKED PORK RIBS WITH FRESH HERBS 43
    SMOKED PORK SIDE RIBS WITH CHIVES 44
    SMOKED SPICY PORK MEDALLIONS 45
    APPLEWOOD SMOKED MANGO PORK QUESADILLAS 46

GRILL LAMB RECIPES 48

    GRILLED LAMB BURGERS... 49
    GRILLED LAMB SANDWICHES.. 50
    LAMB CHOPS 51
    LAMB RIBS RACK 52

Lamb Shank...53

GRILL POULTRY RECIPES...54

Traeger Chile Lime Chicken...55
Traeger Grilled Buffalo Chicken.......................................56
Traeger Sheet Pan Chicken Fajitas....................................57
Traeger Asian Miso Chicken wings....................................58
Yan's Grilled Quarters...59
Cajun Patch Cock Chicken..60

TURKEY, RABBIT AND VEAL...62

Wild Turkey Egg Rolls..63
Trager Smoked Spatchcock Turkey....................................64
Grilled Filet Mignon...65
Buttery Apple Smoked Turkey..66
Smoked Turkey Legs grill..67
Smoked Turkey in Beer Brine...68
Hot Smoked Turkey with Jelly Glaze..................................69

SMOKING RECIPES...70

Smoked Ribs..70
Smoked Pot Roast...71
Smoked Brisket...72
Traeger Smoked Potatoes..73

FISH AND SEAFOOD RECIPES...74

Grilled Lobster Tail...75
Halibut..76
Grilled Salmon...77
Barbeque Shrimp..78
Traeger Grilled Tuna steaks..79
Oyster in Shells..80
Grilled King Crab Legs...81
Cajun Smoked Catfish..82
Smoked Scallops...83
Grilled Tilapia..84
Traeger Salmon with Togarashi.......................................85

VEGETARIAN RECIPES...86

Kale Chips...87
Sweet Potato Fries..88
Potato Fries with Chipotle Peppers...................................89
Traeger Grilled Zucchini...90

SMOKED POTATO SALAD 91

BAKED PARMESAN MUSHROOMS 92

ROASTED SPICY TOMATOES 93

VEGAN RECIPES 94

WOOD PELLET SMOKED MUSHROOMS 95

WOOD PELLET GRILLED ZUCCHINI SQUASH SPEARS 96

RED MEAT RECIPES...98

CHIPOTLE HONEY SMOKED BEEF ROAST 98

LEMON CHILI SMOKED BEEF BRISKET 100

BAKING RECIPES 102

QUICK YEAST DINNER ROLLS 103

BAKED CORNBREAD WITH HONEY BUTTER 104

S'MORES DIP WITH CANDIED PECANS 105

CHEESE AND BREAD.. 106

TRAEGER-GRILL FLATBREAD PIZZA 106

TRAEGER SMOKED NUT MIX 108

APPETIZERS AND SIDES 109

ATOMIC BUFFALO TURDS 109

GRILLED CORN 110

THYME - ROSEMARY MASH POTATOES 111

MORE SIDES.. 112

GRILLED MUSHROOM SKEWERS 112

CAPRESE TOMATO SALAD 114

WATERMELON-CUCUMBER SALAD 115

SNACKS... 116

CORN SALSA 117

NUT MIX ON THE GRILL 118

DESSERT RECIPE.. 120

GRILLED PINEAPPLE WITH CHOCOLATE SAUCE 120

NECTARINE AND NUTELLA SUNDAE 121

CINNAMON SUGAR DONUT HOLES... 122

SAUCES AND RUBS 124

HEAVENLY RABBIT SMOKE... 124

UNCLE JOHNNY'S RUB 125

Fajita Seasoning 126

NUT AND FRUIT RECIPES 128

Smoked Bananas Foster Bread Pudding 128

TRADITIONAL RECIPES 130

Sweet & Spicy Chicken Thighs 130

SAUCES, RUBS, AND MARINATES 132

Classic Kansas City BBQ Sauce 132

RUBS, INJECTABLES, MARINADES, AND MOPS 134

Not-Just-For-Pork Rub 134
Chicken Rub 135

OTHER RECIPES YOU NEVER THOUGHT ABOUT TO GRILL 136

Summer Treat Corn 136
Crunchy Potato Wedges 137
Twice Grilled Potatoes 138
Mouthwatering Cauliflower 139
Super-Addicting Mushrooms 140
Veggie Lover's Burgers 141
Satisfying Veggie Casserole 142
North American Pot Pie 143
Potluck Favorite Baked Beans 144
Traditional English Mac n' Cheese 145
Amazing Irish Soda Bread 146
Native Southern Cornbread 147

CONCLUSION 148

INTRODUCTION

T rager is a grill and smoker-manufacturing company that is based in Oregon and reputed for using all-natural flavored wood pellets. As far as its origins, Joe Traeger wanted to cook a scrumptious meal for his family when he discovered that his gas grill was burned down.

The very next day, he decided to make a grill with wooden pellets to ensure a fire-free barbeque for the entire summer. As time passed, the first grill by Traeger was mass-produced in 1988.

Subsequently, the company released six different models of barbeque grills, apart from rubs, sauces, spices, smokers, and even apparel. Until 2005, Traeger Grills owned the wood pellet stove patent.

So, how does the Traeger grill work? When you turn the appliance on, the motor starts the rotation of a screw-like device, called the auger, which feeds the burn pot. The pellets then are ignited, and exhaust is via the chimney.

Traeger grills are also fitted with air convection that feeds air to the burning pellets. This ensures that the heat is efficiently distributed and the air around the food is filled with smoke. Similar to a convection oven, the heat is moved around the meat.

Some special aspects of the Traeger Grills are:

1. The fuel

Most other types of grills make use of charcoal, natural gas, or propane as a source of fuel. In the case of these fuel sources, the user needs to have a bit of knowledge of the grill type and be present to 'babysit' the grill.

On the other hand, Traeger grills use wood pellets that are all-natural and all-wood. These pellets can burn well in a controlled environment and provide flavorful food. Additionally, these pellets are FDA-approved and safe for home and outdoor uses.

The pellets are available in 14 distinct flavors. They can be used to create a new range of individual flavors and do not harm the environment when burned.

2. Flavor

Traeger pellets are available in 14 different types of pellets like pecan, apple, mesquite, hickory, etc. Apart from infusing delicious flavor to the meat, you can also use them for baking sweets like pie and cookies.

3. No flare-up

There are no flare-ups in roasting, baking, smoking, or grilling when you are using indirect electric heat, not gas. This is because electric heat (indirect) does not lead to flare-ups. The appliances are also not exposed to dripping temperatures.

4. Control of the temperature

One of the best aspects of the Traeger Grill is total control of the temperature. Once you set it, the grill is capable of maintaining consistent heat, even if the weather may not look favorable.

The Traeger grills can be set in 5-degree increments, which is a feature not seen in many grills, especially charcoal and gas ones. All you need to do is cook the food using the recipe and not worry about the appliance dropping down the temperature.

Additionally, since pellets are essentially electric, you are not tied to your grill like a gas grill. For instance, you do not have to keep checking the grill from time-to-time to ensure that the food has not burned.

5. Environmentally-friendly

Grills manufactured by Traeger make use of all-natural and real wood pellets that can burn within a controlled system, thereby offering flavor, ease of use, and convenience.

These grills are also approved by the FDA and the flavors of the pellets can be blended to create a mix of flavors. Additionally, burning these pellets will not cause any harm to the environment, as mentioned before.

The picture of a good time with loved ones, neighbors and friends having a backyard barbeque is a pretty sight, isn't it? Having a smoker-grill and some grilled and smoked recipes are excellent when you have visitors at home, because you can deliver both tasty food and magical moment on a summer night, for example. Hundreds of awesome recipes are available that you can try with a wood pellet smoker-grill! Experiment, improve, or make your own recipes – it is up to you. You can do it fast and easy. But if you want to be safe with the proven and tested ones, by all means do so. These recipes have been known to be just right to the taste and they work every time. A combination of creating a correct impression the first time and every time and enjoying scrumptious food along the way will be your edge.

TRAEGER WOOD PELLET GRILL

Traeger Wood Pellet Grill is a wood pellet grill that has a set of manual controls that allows the user to control the cooking temperature. It differs from other smoker grills such as the Traeger electric smoker and the pellet grills that use a digital control to adjust the temperature. The grill uses a wood pellet fuel that causes it to smoke. The different types of wood pellets that the grill uses to smoke food are Apple wood pellets, Hickory wood pellets, Mesquite wood pellets, Cherry wood pellets, and Alder wood pellets. The wood pellets can be used to smoke chicken, turkey, fish, oysters, cow beef, and many other types of poultry. The wood pellets can be used to smoke other foods such as pizza, vegetables, and other foods. The wood pellets are made using recycled wood materials. The wood pellet grill can also be used to grill foods and bake foods. The grill is easy to use because it's made of a simple design and it doesn't have any complicated elements. The Traeger wood pellet grill is easy to use and can be used indoors as well as outdoors. The user can check the temperature to make sure that the food is cooked perfectly. Most types of the grill can be used both as gas grills and charcoal grills.

One of the popular features of the Traeger wood pellet grill is the result of its smoke from the wood pellet. Many customers are amazed by the wood pellet smoker. There are hundreds of positive and amazing testimonials about the grill. The grill allows users to smoke and grill their food and the meat can be smoked for up to 15 hours. The grill is easy to use, functional, and reliable. The Traeger grill is also very durable because of its body. The body of the grill is made of cast iron. The BBQ grill is easy to install and is easy to maintain. The grill can create smoke by using wood pellets and it can be adjusted to a temperature of about 225 degrees Fahrenheit. The food cooked on the grill has a consistent smoky flavor because of the wood pellets. The grill is an automatic cooker, meaning it conserves the heat that it produces, and it doesn't lose heat.

How It Works

Many people try to grill using real firewood methods while grilling in the Traeger grill. But they do not know how to use Traeger grill with wood pellets. Let's first see how Traeger pellet grill works.

To start with Traeger grill, user has to open the lid and set the temperature at 250 and make the grill smoke by turning it on. It has to be set as 250 for first 30 mins. User also has to turn on the heat of the grill and grill meat or food, which you want to use. The smoke has to be essential for cooking with pellets. If Traeger grill is not important to work with, then user can also set the smoker for working with the Traeger pellets.

It will not work without smoke. So, first thing to do is get the griller hot and the smoker working. The temperature will rise up to 260. The grill grates are placed on the grill so as to let the smoke pass through the meat while cooking. The temperature will rise up to 260, if one is not able to control it, be sure to turn off the barbecue grill. The Traeger grill is very simple to use and it is quite easy to control the temperature.

Once you want to know how to use Traeger grill and smoke, you will be able to find it quite easy and all you need to do is to open the lid and then set the temperature. Switch on the smoke for the first time so that smoke can come out and cook the food.

It is the same as the way how to use Traeger pellet grill for smoking

So, if you want to do BBQs for your family, then Traeger grill is the best choice to use. It has a capacity to hold about seventeen burgers. So, one can easily do a party or BBQ night for quite large crowd. The food will be very tasty, once it is ready with Traeger pellet grill.

Traeger Wood Pellet Grill Vs. Charcoal and Wood Grills

Traeger wood pallets have numerous benefits that other charcoal and gas grill cannot provide. Barbecuing is a great gathering excuse and outdoor activity, but it is a hassle to set. In this day and age where everything is becoming more convenient, this activity should also become easier to deal with as well.

It is easy to start:

To get a charcoal or gas grill to ignite is a hassle, but the fire inside firepot is easy to turn on. It also is much safer as you don't have to stick your hands inside the grill to start the fire.

It's versatile

This grill is not only used for grilling but can be used for different processes of cooking as well. You can bake, roast, smoke, and braise using this device. This also increases the menu at your barbecue gathering.

No burnt areas

Because the cooking process happens by convection mechanism, the entire piece of meat, or whatever your cooking gets cooked evenly. There is also no need to flip around the meat constantly. Also, the drip tray prevents direct fire from hitting your food, so no charring occurs.

More flavor in your dishes

In grilling, nothing beats all-natural hardwood flavor. Professional chefs use them, and now, with ease, so could you. It is not hard to produce a much more delicious juicy meat steak at your home anymore.

Pellets to Use

The dark charcoal type of wood pellets is used to cook food. They are burned to cook food inside it. It is made of a variety of woods like beech, maple, and cherry that has a composition of 15 - 20 percent mesquite, it burns at 1400 degrees. The process to burn wood pellets is very simple. You need to pour it to a box, add in the grill and light it with matchstick, then it will burn to give you the best flavor. The burning wood pellets will provide you the warmth and keep you surrounded with the great and the best natural flavor. This is the burning pellets or the logs that make the grills unique.

Benefits of the Wood Pellet Smoker-Grill

There are several advantages to using a wood pellet smoker-grill. Not only does it enhance the taste of your food, but it also offers several other benefits. Here are some of the biggest benefits of a wood pellet smoker-grill!

Saves Time

It is a no-brainer that anything that saves time as well as effort, especially when it comes to cooking, deserves a warm welcome. One of the biggest advantages of using wood pellet grills is that they save you a lot of time. You can make your smoked dishes much faster and with much more ease and comfort. You can pre-heat them quickly, so you will save a lot of time.

Offers Varied Cooking Options

The best thing about wood pellet smoker-grills is that they give you several options for easy cooking. They are versatile and let you easily experiment with recipes and food. You can try various smoked recipes on the grill and enjoy healthy cooking. The versatility of pellet grills is probably one of their best qualities. This ensures that you can enjoy several lip-smacking recipes in a matter of minutes. In addition, you can use pellet grills to cook all kinds of food, from braised short ribs to chicken wings.

Offers Variety

Another significant advantage of using a wood pellet smoker-grill is that these smokers and grills come in a plethora of sizes and shapes. These grills are built and designed keeping the preferences, needs, and tastes of customers in mind. Therefore, people who are looking for convenient cooking tools can always find something for themselves in wood pellet smokers and grills. You can also choose from a wide range of flavors, such as maple, pecan, hickory, apple, and much more.

Cold Smoking

In addition to wood pellet fire grills and smokers, you can buy cold smokers from some companies. You can cook salmon and cheese dishes in these cold smokers.

Ease of Use

It is common to see many people get intimidated by the idea of using a pellet grill. However, those fears are unfounded. While a pellet grill is quite different from your standard charcoal grills or gas grills, they are surprisingly easy to use.

These grills come with controls that users can set and then simply forget about. They come with several features that make the entire process of grilling a piece of cake.

These grills usually do not require any lighter fluid and they start with a single button. In addition, irrespective of the weather or the temperature outside, these grills can keep the temperature within a 10-degree range of your set temperature. This allows you to cook with zero effort like a pro. These grills are also designed to ensure that you do not overcook or over-smoke your food. Plus, they never flare up. So, there is no need for you to worry about your beautiful eyebrows.

Value

While pellet smokers are slightly more expensive than standard grills, this is for a good reason. As mentioned above, these pieces of equipment offer the perfect combination of a smoker and a grill. They come with solid construction and stainless-steel components. This is precisely why they also come with a nice four-year warranty.

This means that you will not buy these grills for a summer only to dispose of them come winter. In addition, fuel efficiency is another one of their advantages. They come packed with double-wall insulation, which helps them sustain their temperatures better as well as use less fuel.

So, what are you waiting for? If you like to smoke or grill your food, it is not possible to go wrong with a good-quality pellet grill. They provide a wide range of advantages, such as their ease of use and the incredible flavor of your favorite smoked wood. Therefore, these grills are an amazing value for the money.

Keeping this in mind, let us dive right into some amazing tried-and-tested recipes using a wood pellet smoker-grill!

WHAT YOU CAN COOK WITH YOUR TRAEGER

What makes a wood pellet smoker and grill unique is the very thing that fuels it -- wood pellets. Wood pellets are compressed sawdust, made from pine wood, birch wood, fir wood, or crop stalks. Culinary-wise, wood pellets are used mostly as fuel for pellet smokers and grills, although they can also be used for household heating. What makes wood pellets for cooking special, though, is that they come in flavors. And speaking of flavors, here is a quick wood pellet flavor guide for you:

Apple & Cherry Pellets: These pellets possess a smoky, mild, sweet flavor. They can enhance mild meat and are usually the go-to flavor for cooking pork or poultry. Despite being able to produce great Smoke, these pellets are very mild.

Alder Pellets: This type of pellet is mild and neutral, but with some sweetness in it. If you're looking for something that provides a good amount of Smoke but won't overpower delicate meat like chicken and fish, this is the flavor to go to.

Hickory Pellets: Hickory pellets produce a rich, Smokey, and bacon-like flavor. These are the pellets that are widely used for barbecue. Since this type of pellet is rich and Smokey, it can tend to be overwhelming. If that is the case, consider mixing it with apple or oak pellets.

Maple Pellets: If you are looking for something that is mild and comes with a hint of sweetness, maple pellets are the best option for you. They are great to use on turkey or pork.

Mesquite Pellets: A favorite option for Texas BBQ, mesquite pellets, is characterized by a strong, spicy, and tangy flavor.

Oak Pellets: Oak pellets come in between apple and Hickory. They are a bit stronger than the former and a bit milder than the latter and are an excellent choice when you're cooking fish or vegetables.

Pecan Pellets: Pecan is an all-time favorite. It's very similar to Hickory, but with a touch of Vanilla, nutty flavor. The perfect pellets for beef and chicken, pecan pellets are very palatable and suits all of

Qualities of a Good Brand of Wood Pellets

With the hundreds of different wood pellets' varieties and brands, it is often difficult to identify which brand to consider. If you are not sure what brand to opt for, it might help try at least the top three brands you know of and compare their efficiency. Appearance: The first factor to consider when choosing a brand of wood pellets is the appearance of the pellets. After using wood pellets for some time, you will be able to tell and judge their quality simply by how they appear. The first thing to check is the length of the pellets. Brands adhere to certain standards, so this is not a concern. Nevertheless, you need to understand that when it comes to pellet fuels, length matters, affecting the performance of the pellets. The dust you will find in the packaging is also another to consider. It is normal to see fines once you open the bag, but if there are an unusual number of fines, it means the pellets aren't of good quality.

Texture: The texture of the pellets is another thing. Wood pellets have a particular texture in them. If you feel that the pellets are smooth and shiny, it means they are of good quality. The same is true if the pellets do not have cracks. If the pellets are too rough with unusual racks on the surface, it means the pellets are bad. This is usually a result of incorrect pressing ratio and moisture content of the raw materials used in making the pellets. Smell: Wood pellets are made by exposing them to high temperatures within a sealed space. During the process, the lignin contained in the biomass material is mixed with other elements, producing a smell of burnt fresh wood. If the pellets smell bad, there is a big chance they have not been appropriately processed or contain impure, raw material. Aside from the appearance, texture, and smell of the wood pellets, another way to check their quality is to see how they react with water. Place a handful of pellets in a bowl of water and allow them to settle for several minutes. If the pellets dissolve in the water and expand quickly, this means they are of good quality. On the other hand, if the pellets do not dissolve within minutes but instead expand and become hard, it means they are of bad quality. Finally, try burning some of the pellets, as well. If the wood pellets are of excellent quality, the flame they produce will be bright and brown. If the flame they make, on the other hand, is dark in color, it means the quality of the pellets is not good. Also, good-quality pellets produce a little ash, so if the pellets leave you with many residues, it is a sign that the pellets are bad.

Cooking Temperatures, Times, and Doneness:

With so many recipes to try with your pellet grill, it is easy to get overwhelmed right away. One important thing to keep in mind is that lower temperatures produce Smoke, while higher temperatures do not. Follow this useful guide below to know the temperature and time required to get the perfectly flavored meat each time.

- Beef briskets are best cooked at 250 degrees using the smoke setting for at least 4 hours by itself and covered with foil for another 4 hours.

- Pork ribs should be cooked at 275 degrees on the smoke setting for 3 hours and covered with foil for another 2-3 hours.

- Steaks require 400-450 degrees for about 10 minutes on each side.

- Turkey can be cooked at 375 degrees for 20 minutes per pound of meat. For smoked turkey, the heat settings should be around 180-225 degrees for 10-12 hours or until the turkeys inside reaches 165 degrees.

- Chicken breasts can be cooked at 400-450 degrees for 15 minutes on each side.

- A whole chicken cooks at 400-450 degrees for 1.5 hours or until the internal temperature reaches 165 degrees.

- Bacon and Sausage can be cooked at 425 degrees for 5-8 minutes on each side.

- Hamburgers should be cooked at 350 degrees for at least 8 minutes for each side.

- You can smoke salmon for 1-1.5 hours and finish with a high setting for 2-3 minutes on each side.

- Shrimps cook at 400-450 degrees for 3-5 minutes on each side. If you prefer a smokier flavor, set the temperature at 225 degrees for about 30 minutes.

Wood to Meat Pairing Chart

FLAVOR	BEEF	PORK	SEAFOOD	LAMB	GAME MEAT
Apple	X	X	X		
Alder		X		X	
Hickory	X	X		X	X
Mesquite	X	X	X		
Oak		X		X	X
Pecan	X	X		X	X

CLEANING AND MAINTENANCE

Alll equipment, including a grill smoker, needs to be taken care of. Especially if you're serious about smoking and want your equipment to last.

The main difference between smokers and grills is the temperature at which the food is cooked. A smoker cooks food at a low temperature (about 225 degrees F) and a grill cooks it at 300 degrees F or higher. The reason this is important is that when food is cooked at a lower temperature, the metal needs to be taken better care of that the metal of grills that use high heat. With a grill, the high heat can incinerate most cooking grease left behind in the fire chamber while the lower heat of the smoker is unable to do that, so the grease remains.

3 rules when using a smoker:

A brand-new smoker needs to be seasoned before use

To season a smoker, you first need to coat the inside surface with some kind of cooking oil or bacon grease.

When that oil is heated, it will seep into all the pores of the metal surface of the smoker. This will create a barrier that prevents rusting.

You need to heat the smoker to a temperature of about 250-275 degrees F. Don't goes above this temperature as you may damage the paint. You can use charcoal but it's better to use the sort of fuel you plan to use for smoking food. Keep the smoker at this temperature for 2-3 hours.

Seasoning is essential because it destroys all the chemicals used during the manufacturing process so even if the instruction book does not insist on seasoning, it's better to fire up your smoker than not. That way you'll be sure your food is free of toxins.

A smoker will occasionally have to be repaired and repainted

From time to time, even if you are not using it very often, your smoker will need to be cleaned. Remove all the rust by scrubbing it with a wire brush and sandpaper. Clean it thoroughly and repaint it with heat resistant barbecue paint. A good-quality smoker can last many decades, i.e. a lifetime, provided you take good care of it. Don't forget that the state of your smoker affects the taste of the food you prepare in it. Therefore, routine maintenance is essential.

It needs to be cleaned after each and every use

Taking care of your smoker means you will have to keep it clean by removing the ash and not allow food build-up. However, although a smoker requires occasional scrubbing, the protective coating must not be damaged so you should never scrub the smoker down to the bare metal.

If you've had it for a long time or use it often, you may need to thoroughly clean it out and season it from time to time. To prevent rusting, you need to maintain the smoky, oily surface over the metal.

Ash should never be allowed to remain in the smoker after it's been used, as it can absorb water and lead to rusting. Large deposits of grease trapped against the metal need to be scraped gently. A clean and looked-after smoker not only has a longer life but it also makes your food taste better.

TIPS TO SUCCEED

Tips and Tricks for Using Your Traeger Grill

I f you are looking for some tips and tricks that can help you better utilize your Traeger grill, they are listed for you. If you already have the appliance, you are already on the sweet side of life. Whether you are a grill newbie or a master, there are always things that you can learn to become the ultimate grill and smoker master.

Some of the top tricks, tips, and hacks that can make your barbequing, smoking, and grilling experience better include:

1. Always use disposable drip bucket liners

If you get tired of cleaning up that slimy residue every time you decide to grill or smoke some steak or are prone to bumping the bucket off accidentally when putting on the cover, it is recommended that you look for bucket liners - disposable ones of course. With the help of these disposable drip bucket liners, cleaning will become much easier.

2. Grill lights to light the way

If you plan on cooking at night or are always bumping around the grill in the dark, you can look for some grill lights. If you are a serious smoker but are busy dealing with the headlamp or flashlight, these grill lights will come in very handy.

No wonder this device is one of the top-sellers on several online shopping sites. The grill lights are fitted with a magnetic base and can clamp and bend according to the shape of the grill.

3. Drip tray liners for easier cleaning

If you want to get serious, then it is time to dump the aluminum foil. Once you have the drip tray liners, you will not have to deal with wadded up, oily, blackened, or small tears in the foil.

The overall idea here is to make the cleaning process easier so that you can redirect your focus on the more important things, such as smoking and grilling.

4. Meat temperature and meat smoking magnets to measure the temperature accurately

One of the worst things that can happen while grilling and smoking meat is guessing the cooking temperature. With the help of meat smoking and temperature magnets, you can now leave all the frantic web searches behind.

With these devices, you will know the internal temperature that you need to cook meat safely. Then, you will always have perfectly cooked pieces of meat all the time.

5. Wireless thermometer or Tappecue for the perfect temperature

You have already spent hundreds of dollars on a perfect grill. However, you can still end up spending tens and thousands of dollars more each time you decide to cook on it.

If you want to protect your important investment from harm, you need to ensure that you do not have to 'peek' while cooking. With the Tappecue, you will get the internal temperature that you are looking for.

6. Swap out pellets with bucket head vacuum

Imagine that you need to move from the apple to the hickory flavor. However, you see that the grill is more than half-full of apple pellets. What can do you in this scenario? Of course, you can choose to wait until the pellets cool down and then remove them. Another solution to this issue is using a bucket head vacuum.

Once done, you will be left with storage that you can use any time. Additionally, you do not even need a specialized bucket for this purpose; you can use a simple bucket and storage lid kit that is fitted with a filter.

7. Add extra smoke on any type of cooking with an A-maze-n Smoker Tube

If you love smoking, you should definitely buy a dedicated smoker tube – like the A-maze-n Smoker Tube. Known for its great simplicity, this tube is one of the best tools for a seasoned smoker. All you need to do is to add some pellets and light it at just one end. Then, leave it on the grates.

A smoker tube is a great option for cold smoking fish, nuts, and cheese; of course, it can also be used for some extra smoke on meats, like brisket, pulled pork, etc.

GRILL BEEF RECIPES

Beef Tenderloin

Preparation Time: 10 minutes

Cooking Time: 1 hour 19 minutes

Servings: 12

Ingredients:

- 1 (5-pound) beef tenderloin, trimmed
- Kosher salt, as required
- ¼ cup olive oil
- Freshly ground black pepper, as required

Directions:

1. With kitchen strings, tie the tenderloin at 7-8 places.
2. Season tenderloin with kosher salt generously.
3. With a plastic wrap, cover the tenderloin and keep aside at room temperature for about 1 hour.
4. Preheat the Z Grills Traeger Grill & Smoker on grill setting to 225-250 degrees F.
5. Now, coat tenderloin with oil evenly and season with black pepper.
6. Arrange tenderloin onto the grill and cook for about 55-65 minutes.
7. Now, place cooking grate directly over hot coals and sear tenderloin for about 2 minutes per side.
8. Remove the tenderloin from the grill and place onto a cutting board for about 10-15 minutes before serving.
9. With a sharp knife, cut the tenderloin into desired-sized slices and serve.

Nutrition: Calories 425 Total Fat 21.5 g Saturated Fat 7.2 g Cholesterol 174 mg Sodium 123 mg Total Carbs 0 g Fiber 0 g Sugar 0 g Protein 54.7 g

Mustard Beef Short Ribs

Preparation Time: 15 minutes

Cooking Time: 3 hours

Servings: 6

Ingredients:

For Mustard Sauce:

- 1 cup prepared yellow mustard
- ¼ cup red wine vinegar
- ¼ cup dill pickle juice
- 2 tablespoons soy sauce
- 2 tablespoons Worcestershire sauce
- 1 teaspoon ground ginger
- 1 teaspoon granulated garlic

For Spice Rub:

- 2 tablespoons salt
- 2 tablespoons freshly ground black pepper
- 1 tablespoon white cane sugar
- 1 tablespoon granulated garlic

For Ribs:

- 6 (14-ounce) (4-5-inch long) beef short ribs

Directions:

1. Preheat the Z Grills Traeger Grill & Smoker on smoke setting to 230-250 degrees F, using charcoal.
2. For sauce: in a bowl, mix together all ingredients.
3. For rub: in a small bowl, mix together all ingredients.
4. Coat the ribs with sauce generously and then sprinkle with spice rub evenly.
5. Place the ribs onto the grill over indirect heat, bone side down.
6. Cook for about 1-1½ hours.
7. Flip the side and cook for about 45 minutes.
8. Flip the side and cook for about 45 minutes more.
9. Remove the ribs from grill and place onto a cutting board for about 10 minutes before serving.
10. With a sharp knife, cut the ribs into equal sized individual pieces and serve.

Nutrition: Calories 867 Total Fat 37.5 g Saturated Fat 13.7 g Cholesterol 361 mg Sodium 3462mg Total Carbs 7.7 g Fiber 2.1 g Sugar 3.6 g Protein 117.1 g

Sweet & Spicy Beef Brisket

Preparation Time: 10 minutes

Cooking Time: 7 hours

Servings: 10

Ingredients:

- 1 cup paprika
- ¾ cup sugar
- 3 tablespoons garlic salt
- 3 tablespoons onion powder
- 1 tablespoon celery salt
- 1 tablespoon lemon pepper
- 1 tablespoon ground black pepper
- 1 teaspoon cayenne pepper
- 1 teaspoon mustard powder
- ½ teaspoon dried thyme, crushed
- 1 (5-6-pound) beef brisket, trimmed

Directions:

1. In a bowl, place all ingredients except for beef brisket and mix well.
2. Rub the brisket with spice mixture generously.
3. With a plastic wrap, cover the brisket and refrigerate overnight.
4. Preheat the Z Grills Traeger Grill & Smoker on grill setting to 250 degrees F.
5. Place the brisket onto grill over indirect heat and cook for about 3-3½ hours.
6. Flip and cook for about 3-3½ hours more.
7. Remove the brisket from grill and place onto a cutting board for about 10-15 minutes before slicing.
8. With a sharp knife, cut the brisket in desired sized slices and serve.

Nutrition: Calories 536 Total Fat 15.6 g Saturated Fat 5.6 g Cholesterol 203 mg Sodium 158 mg Total Carbs 24.8 g Fiber 4.5 g Sugar 17.4 g Protein 71.1 g

Brandy Beef Tenderloin

Preparation Time: 15 minutes

Cooking Time: 2 hours 2 minutes

Servings: 6

Ingredients:

For Brandy Butter:

- ½ cup butter
- 1 ounce brandy

For Brandy Sauce:

- 2 ounces brandy
- 8 garlic cloves, minced
- ¼ cup mixed fresh herbs (parsley, rosemary and thyme), chopped
- 2 teaspoons honey
- 2 teaspoons hot English mustard

For Tenderloin:

- 1 (2-pound) center-cut beef tenderloin
- Salt and cracked black peppercorns, as required

Directions:

1. Preheat the Z Grills Traeger Grill & Smoker on grill setting to 230 degrees F.
2. For brandy butter: in a pan, melt butter over medium-low heat.
3. Stir in brandy and remove from heat.
4. Set aside, covered to keep warm.
5. For brandy sauce: in a bowl, add all ingredients and mix until well combined.
6. Season the tenderloin with salt and black peppercorns generously.
7. Coat tenderloin with brandy sauce evenly.
8. With a baster-injector, inject tenderloin with brandy butter.
9. Place the tenderloin onto the grill and cook for about ½-2 hours, injecting with brandy butter occasionally.
10. Remove the tenderloin from grill and place onto a cutting board for about 10-15 minutes before serving.
11. With a sharp knife, cut the tenderloin into desired-sized slices and serve.

Nutrition: Calories 496 Total Fat 29.3 g Saturated Fat 15 g Cholesterol 180 mg Sodium 240 mg Total Carbs 4.4 g Fiber 0.7 g Sugar 2 g Protein 44.4 g

Beef Rump Roast

Preparation Time: 10 minutes

Cooking Time: 6 hours

Servings: 8

Ingredients:

- 1 teaspoon smoked paprika
- 1 teaspoon cayenne pepper
- 1 teaspoon onion powder
- 1 teaspoon garlic powder
- Salt and ground black pepper, as required
- 3 pounds beef rump roast
- ¼ cup Worcestershire sauce

Directions:

1. Preheat the Z Grills Traeger Grill & Smoker on smoke setting to 200 degrees F, using charcoal.
2. In a bowl, mix together all spices.
3. Coat the rump roast with Worcestershire sauce evenly and then, rub with spice mixture generously.
4. Place the rump roast onto the grill and cook for about 5-6 hours.
5. Remove the roast from the grill and place onto a cutting board for about 10-15 minutes before serving.
6. With a sharp knife, cut the roast into desired-sized slices and serve.

Nutrition: Calories 252 Total Fat 9.1 g Saturated Fat 3 g Cholesterol 113 mg Sodium 200 mg Total Carbs 2.3 g Fiber 0.2 g Sugar 1.8 g Protein 37.8 g

Herbed Prime Rib Roast

Preparation Time: 10 minutes

Cooking Time: 3 hours 50 minutes

Servings: 10

Ingredients:

- 1 (5-pound) prime rib roast
- Salt, as required
- 5 tablespoons olive oil
- 2 teaspoons dried thyme, crushed
- 2 teaspoons dried rosemary, crushed
- 2 teaspoons garlic powder
- 1 teaspoon onion powder
- 1 teaspoon paprika
- ½ teaspoon cayenne pepper
- Ground black pepper, as required

Directions:

1. Season the roast with salt generously.
2. With a plastic wrap, cover the roast and refrigerate for about 24 hours.
3. In a bowl, mix together remaining ingredients and set aside for about 1 hour.
4. Rub the roast with oil mixture from both sides evenly.
5. Arrange the roast in a large baking sheet and refrigerate for about 6-12 hours.
6. Preheat the Z Grills Traeger Grill & Smoker on smoke setting to 225-230 degrees F, using pecan wood chips.
7. Place the roast onto the grill and cook for about 3-3½ hours.
8. Meanwhile, preheat the oven to 500 degrees F.
9. Remove the roast from grill and place onto a large baking sheet.
10. Place the baking sheet in oven and roast for about 15-20 minutes.
11. Remove the roast from oven and place onto a cutting board for about 10-15 minutes before serving.
12. With a sharp knife, cut the roast into desired-sized slices and serve.

Nutrition: Calories 605 Total Fat 47.6 g Saturated Fat 17.2 g Cholesterol 135 mg Sodium 1285

Spicy Chuck Roast

Preparation Time: 10 minutes

Cooking Time: 4½ hours

Servings: 8

Ingredients:

- 2 tablespoons onion powder
- 2 tablespoons garlic powder
- 1 tablespoon red chili powder
- 1 tablespoon cayenne pepper
- Salt and ground black pepper, as required
- 1 (3 pound) beef chuck roast
- 16 fluid ounces warm beef broth

Directions:

1. Preheat the Z Grills Traeger Grill & Smoker on grill setting to 250 degrees F.
2. In a bowl, mix together spices, salt and black pepper.
3. Rub the chuck roast with spice mixture evenly.
4. Place the rump roast onto the grill and cook for about 1½ hours per side.
5. Now, arrange chuck roast in a steaming pan with beef broth.
6. With a piece of foil, cover the pan and cook for about 2-3 hours.
7. Remove the chuck roast from grill and place onto a cutting board for about 20 minutes before slicing.
8. With a sharp knife, cut the chuck roast into desired-sized slices and serve.

Nutrition: Calories 645 Total Fat 48 g Saturated Fat 19 g Cholesterol 175 mg Sodium 329 mg Total Carbs 4.2 g Fiber 1 g Sugar 1.4 g Protein 46.4 g

GRILL PORK RECIPES

Smoked Avocado Pork Ribs

Preparation Time: 20 Minutes

Cooking Time: 3 Hours

Servings: 5

Ingredients:

- 2 lbs. of pork spare ribs
- 1 cup of avocado oil
- One teaspoon of garlic powder
- One teaspoon of onion powder
- One teaspoon of sweet pepper flakes
- Salt and pepper, to taste

Directions:

1. In a bowl, combine the avocado oil, garlic salt, garlic powder, onion powder, sweet pepper flakes, and salt and pepper.
2. Place pork chops in a shallow container and pour evenly avocado mixture.
3. Cover and refrigerate for at least 4 hours or overnight.
4. Start pellet grill on, lid open until the fire is established (4-5 minutes).
5. Increase the temperature to 225 and pre-heat for 10 - 15 minutes.
6. Arrange pork chops on the grill rack and smoke for 3 to 4 hours.
7. Transfer pork chops on serving plate, let them rest for 15 minutes, and serve.

Nutrition: Calories: 677 call Carbohydrates: 0.9g Fat: 64g Fiber: 0.14g Protein: 28.2g

Smoked Honey - Garlic Pork Chops

Preparation Time: 15 Minutes

Cooking Time: 60 Minutes

Servings: 4

Ingredients:

- 1/4 cup of lemon juice freshly squeezed
- 1/4 cup honey (preferably a darker honey)
- Three cloves garlic, minced
- Two tablespoons of soy sauce (or tamari sauce)
- Salt and pepper to taste
- 24 ounces center-cut pork chops boneless

Directions:

1. Combine honey, lemon juice, soy sauce, garlic, and salt and pepper in a bowl.
2. Place pork in a container and pour marinade over pork.
3. Cover and marinate in a fridge overnight.
4. Remove pork from marinade and pat dry on kitchen paper towel. (Reserve marinade)
5. Start your pellet on Smoke with the lid open until the fire is established (4 - 5 minutes).
6. Increase temperature to 450 and preheat, lid closed, for 10 - 15 minutes.
7. Arrange the pork chops on the grill racks and smoke for about one hour (depending on the thickness)
8. In the meantime, heat the remaining marinade in a small saucepan over medium heat to simmer.
9. Transfer pork chops on a serving plate, pour with the marinade, and serve hot.

Nutrition: Calories: 301.5 call Carbohydrates: 17g Fat: 6.5g Fiber: 0.2g Protein: 41g

Smoked Pork Burgers

Preparation Time: 15 Minutes

Cooking Time: 1 Hour and 45 Minutes

Servings: 4

Ingredients:

- 2 lb. ground pork
- 1/2 of onion finely chopped
- 2 Tablespoon fresh sage, chopped
- One teaspoon garlic powder
- One teaspoon cayenne pepper
- Salt and pepper to taste

Directions:

1. Start the pellet grill on SMOKE wait until the fire is established.
2. Set the temperature to 225 and warm-up, lid closed, for 10 to 15 minutes.
3. In a bowl, combine ground pork with all remaining ingredients.
4. Use your hands to mix thoroughly—form mixture into eight evenly burgers.
5. Place the hamburgers on the racks.
6. Smoke the burgers for 60 minutes until they reach an internal temperature of 150 to 160.
7. Serve hot.

Nutrition: Calories: 588.7 call Carbohydrates: 1g Fat: 48.2g Fiber: 0.5g Protein: 38.4g

Smoked Pork Chops Marinated with Tarragon

Preparation Time: 20 Minutes

Cooking Time: 3 Hours

Servings: 4

Ingredients:

- 1/2 cup olive oil
- 4 Tablespoon of fresh tarragon chopped
- Two teaspoons fresh thyme, chopped
- Salt and grated black pepper
- Two teaspoon apple cider vinegar
- Four pork chops or fillets

Directions:

1. Whisk the olive oil, tarragon, thyme, salt, pepper, apple cider, and stir well.
2. Place the pork chops in a container and pour it with a tarragon mixture.
3. Refrigerate for 2 hours.
4. Start pellet grill on, lid open, until the discharge is established (4-5 minutes). Increase the temperature to 225 and allow to pre-heat, lid closed, for 10 - 15 minutes.
5. Remove chops from marinade and pat dry on kitchen towel.
6. Arrange pork chops on the grill rack and smoke for 2 to 3 hours.
7. Transfer chops on a serving platter and lets it rest 15 minutes before serving.

Nutrition: Calories: 528.8 Cal Carbohydrates: 0.6g Fat: 35g Fiber: 0.14g Protein: 51g

Smoked Pork Cutlets in Citrus-Herbs Marinade

Preparation Time: 4 Hours

Cooking Time: 1 Hour and 45 Minutes

Servings: 4

Ingredients:

- Four pork cutlets
- One fresh orange juice
- Two large lemons freshly squeezed
- Ten twigs of coriander chopped
- 2 Tablespoon of fresh parsley finely chopped
- Three cloves of garlic minced
- 2 Tablespoon of olive oil
- Salt and ground black pepper

Directions:

1. Place the pork cutlets in a large container along with all remaining ingredients; toss to cover well.
2. Refrigerate at least 4 hours or overnight.
3. When ready, remove the pork cutlets from marinade and pat dry on a kitchen towel.
4. Start pellet grill on, lid open until the fire is established (4-5 minutes). Upsurge the temperature to 250 and allow to pre-heat, lid closed, for 10 - 15 minutes.
5. Place pork cutlets on grill grate and smoke for 1 1/2 hours.
6. Serve hot.

Nutrition: Calories: 260 Cal Carbohydrates: 5g Fat: 12g Fiber: 0.25g Protein: 32.2g

Smoked Pork Cutlets with Caraway and Dill

Preparation Time: 4 Hours

Cooking Time: 1 Hour and 45 Minutes

Servings: 4

Ingredients:

- Four pork cutlets
- Two lemons freshly squeezed
- Two tablespoons fresh parsley finely chopped
- 1 Tablespoon of ground caraway
- 3 Tablespoon of fresh dill finely chopped
- 1/4 cup of olive oil
- Salt and ground black pepper

Directions:

1. Place the pork cutlets in a large resealable bag and all remaining ingredients; shake to combine well.
2. Refrigerate for at least 4 hours.
3. Remove the pork cutlets from marinade and pat dry on a kitchen towel.
4. Start the pellet grill (recommended maple pellet) on SMOKE with the lid open until the fire is established.
5. Set the temperature to 250 and preheat for 10 to 15 minutes.
6. Arrange pork cutlets on the grill rack and smoke for about 1 1/2 hours.
7. Allow cooling at room temperature before serving.

Nutrition: Calories: 308 Cal Carbohydrates: 2.4g Fat: 18.5g Fiber: 0.36g Protein: 32g

Smoked Pork Loin in Sweet-Beer Marinade

Preparation Time: 15 Minutes

Cooking Time: 3 Hours

Servings: 6

Ingredients:

Marinade

- One onion finely diced
- 1/4 cup honey (preferably a darker honey)
- 1 1/2 cups of dark beer
- 4 Tablespoon of mustard
- 1 Tablespoon fresh thyme finely chopped
- Salt and pepper

Pork

- 3 1/2 lbs. of pork loin

Directions:

1. Combine all fixings for the marinade in a bowl.
2. Place the pork along with marinade mixture in a container, and refrigerate overnight.
3. Remove the pork from the marinade and dry on a kitchen towel.
4. Prepare the grill on Smoke with the lid open until the fire is established.
5. Set the temperature to 250F and preheat, lid closed, for 10 to 15 minutes.
6. Place the meat on the grill rack and smoke until the pork's internal temperature is at least 145-150 (medium-rare), 2-1/2 to 3 hours.
7. Remove meat from the smoker and let rest for 15 minutes before slicing.
8. Serve hot or cold.

Nutrition: Calories: 444.6 Cal Carbohydrates: 17g Fat: 12.7g Fiber: 0.8g Protein: 60.5g

Smoked Pork Ribs with Fresh Herbs

Preparation Time: 20 Minutes

Cooking Time: 3 Hours

Servings: 6

Ingredients:

- 1/4 cup olive oil
- 1 Tablespoon garlic minced
- 1 Tablespoon crushed fennel seeds
- One teaspoon of fresh basil leaves finely chopped
- One teaspoon fresh parsley finely chopped
- One teaspoon fresh rosemary finely chopped
- One teaspoon fresh sage finely chopped
- Salt and ground black pepper to taste
- 3 lbs. pork rib roast bone-in

Directions:

1. Combine the olive oil, garlic, fennel seeds, parsley, sage, rosemary, salt, and pepper in a bowl; stir well.
2. Coat each chop on equal sides with the herb mixture.
3. Start the pellet grill (recommended hickory pellet) on SMOKE with the lid open until the fire is established. Set the temperature to 225 and heat up, lid closed, for 10 to 15 minutes.
4. Smoke the ribs for 3 hours.
5. Transfer the ribs to a platter and serve hot.

Nutrition: Calories: 459.2 Cal Carbohydrates: 0.6g Fat: 31.3g Fiber: 0.03g Protein: 41g

Smoked Pork Side Ribs with Chives

Preparation Time: 15 Minutes

Cooking Time: 3 Hours and 20 Minutes

Servings: 6

Ingredients:

- 1/3 cup of olive oil (or garlic-infused olive oil)
- 3 Tablespoon of ketchup
- 3 Tablespoon chives finely chopped
- 3 lbs. of pork side ribs
- Salt and black pepper to taste

Directions:

1. In a bowl, stir together olive oil, finely chopped chives, ketchup, salt, and pepper.
2. Cut pork into individual ribs and generously coat with chives mixture.
3. Flinch the pellet grill on SMOKE with the lid open until the discharge is established.
4. Set the temperature to 250 and preheat for 10 to 15 minutes.
5. Arrange pork chops on the grill rack and smoke for about 3 to 4 hours.
6. Allow resting 15 minutes before serving.

Nutrition: Calories: 689.7 Cal Carbohydrates: 2g Fat: 65g Fiber: 0.1g Protein: 35.2g

Smoked Spicy Pork Medallions

Preparation Time: 15 Minutes

Cooking Time: 1 Hour and 45 Minutes

Servings: 6

Ingredients:

- 2 lb. pork medallions
- 3/4 cup chicken stock
- 1/2 cup tomato sauce (organic)
- 2 Tablespoon of smoked hot paprika (or to taste)
- 2 Tablespoon of fresh basil finely chopped
- 1 Tablespoon oregano
- Salt and pepper to taste

Directions:

1. In a bowl, blend the chicken stock, tomato sauce, paprika, oregano, salt, and pepper.
2. Brush bigheartedly over the outside of the tenderloin.
3. Twitch the pellet grill on Smoke with the lid open until the fire is established (4 to 5 minutes). Set the temperature to 250 and preheat, lid closed, for 10 to 15 minutes.
4. Place the pork on the grill grate and smoke until the pork's internal temperature is at minimum medium-rare (about 145) for 1 1/2 hours.
5. Let meat rest for 15 minutes and serve.

Nutrition: Calories: 364.2 Cal Carbohydrates: 4g Fat: 14.4g Fiber: 2g Protein: 52.4g

Applewood Smoked Mango Pork Quesadillas

Preparation Time: 10 Minutes

Cooking Time: 15 Minutes

Servings: 4

Ingredients:

- One tablespoon olive oil
- 1.7 pounds Smithfield Applewood Smoked Bacon Pork Loin Filet cut into little scaled-down pieces
- One teaspoon chipotle stew powder pretty much to your taste
- One teaspoon smoked paprika
- 4-inch flour tortillas 6-8
- One ready yet firm mango, stripped + diced
- 1 cup cooked rice or quinoa
- 2 cups destroyed sharp cheddar
- Cherry tomato salsa:
- 2 cup cherry tomatoes
- One jalapeno seeded + hacked
- 1/4 cup new basil cleaved
- 1/4 cup fresh cilantro cleaved
- Juice from 1/2 a lime
- Salt to taste

Directions:

1. Warmth a heavy skillet over medium heat and include olive oil, contain the pork, and season with chipotle bean stew pepper and paprika. Cook, regularly mixing until the pork is caramelized, all finished around 8 minutes. Expel from the warmth. Expel the pork to a plate.
2. Utilizing a similar skillet, over medium warmth, include a touch of olive oil. Spot 4 tortillas down on a perfect counter, sprinkle each with destroyed cheddar, at that point equally appropriate the rice, and top with the hacked mango pieces. Presently include the pork, cut into little scaled-down pieces. Sprinkle with somewhat more of the cheddar. Spot the tortilla onto the hot frying pan or skillet and spread with the other tortilla. Cook until the base is firm and brilliant dark-colored. At that point, tenderly flip and cook for another 2-3 minutes until fresh and bright.
3. Present with the tomato salsa and cut avocado.

Nutrition: Calories: 477 Cal Carbohydrates: 4.5g Fat: 14g Fiber: 2.4g Protein: 50g

GRILL LAMB RECIPES

Grilled Lamb Burgers

Preparation Time: 10 minutes

Cooking Time: 15 minutes

Servings: 5

Ingredients:

- 1 1/4 pounds of ground lamb.
- 1 egg.
- 1 teaspoon of dried oregano.
- 1 teaspoon of dry sherry.
- 1 teaspoon of white wine vinegar.
- 4 minced cloves of garlic.
- Red pepper
- 1/2 cup of chopped green onions.
- 1 tablespoon of chopped mint.
- 2 tablespoons of chopped cilantro.
- 2 tablespoons of dry bread crumbs.
- 1/8 teaspoon of salt to taste.
- 1/4 teaspoon of ground black pepper to taste.
- 5 hamburger buns.

Directions:

1. Preheat a Wood Pellet Smoker or Grill to 350-450 degrees F then grease it grates.
2. Using a large mixing bowl, add in all the ingredients on the list aside from the buns then mix properly to combine with clean hands.
3. Make about five patties out of the mixture then set aside.
4. Place the lamb patties on the preheated grill and cook for about seven to nine minutes turning only once until an inserted thermometer reads 160 degrees F.
5. Serve the lamb burgers on the hamburger, add your favorite toppings and enjoy.

Nutrition: Calories: 376 Cal Fat: 18.5 g Carbohydrates: 25.4 g Protein: 25.5 g Fiber: 1.6 g

Grilled Lamb Sandwiches

Preparation Time: 5 minutes

Cooking Time: 50 minutes

Servings: 6

Ingredients:

- 1 (4 pounds) boneless lamb.
- 1 cup of raspberry vinegar.
- 2 tablespoons of olive oil.
- 1 tablespoon of chopped fresh thyme.
- 2 pressed garlic cloves.
- 1/4 teaspoon of salt to taste.
- 1/4 teaspoon of ground pepper.
- Sliced bread.

Directions:

1. Using a large mixing bowl, add in the raspberry vinegar, oil, and thyme then mix properly to combine. Add in the lamb, toss to combine then let it sit in the refrigerator for about eight hours or overnight.
2. Next, discard the marinade the season the lamb with salt and pepper to taste. Preheat a Wood Pellet Smoker and grill t0 400-500 degrees F, add in the seasoned lamb and grill for about thirty to forty minutes until it attains a temperature of 150 degrees F.
3. Once cooked, let the lamb cool for a few minutes, slice as desired then serve on the bread with your favorite topping.

Nutrition: Calories: 407 Cal Fat: 23 g Carbohydrates: 26 g Protein: 72 g Fiber: 2.3 g

Lamb Chops

Preparation Time: 10 minutes

Cooking Time: 12 minutes

Servings: 6

Ingredients:

- 6 (6-ounce) lamb chops
- 3 tablespoons olive oil
- Ground black pepper

Directions:

1. Preheat the pallet grill to 450 degrees F.
2. Coat the lamb chops with oil and then, season with salt and black pepper evenly.
3. Arrange the chops in pallet grill grate and cook for about 4-6 minutes per side.

Nutrition: Calories: 376 Cal Fat: 19.5 g Carbohydrates: 0 g Protein: 47.8 g Fiber: 0 g

Lamb Ribs Rack

Preparation Time: 10 minutes

Cooking Time: 2 hours

Servings: 2

Ingredients:

- 2 tablespoons fresh sage
- 2 tablespoons fresh rosemary
- 2 tablespoons fresh thyme
- 2 peeled garlic cloves
- 1 tablespoon honey
- Black pepper
- ¼ cup olive oil
- 1 (1½-pound) trimmed rack lamb ribs

Directions:

1. Combine all ingredients
2. While motor is running, slowly add oil and pulse till a smooth paste is formed.
3. Coat the rib rack with paste generously and refrigerate for about 2 hours.
4. Preheat the pallet grill to 225 degrees F.
5. Arrange the rib rack in pallet grill and cook for about 2 hours.
6. Remove the rib rack from pallet grill and transfer onto a cutting board for about 10-15 minutes before slicing.
7. With a sharp knife, cut the rib rack into equal sized individual ribs and serve.

Nutrition: Calories: 826 Cal Fat: 44.1 g Carbohydrates: 5.4 g Protein: 96.3 g Fiber: 1 g

Lamb Shank

Preparation Time: 10 minutes

Cooking Time: 4 hours

Servings: 6

Ingredients:

- 8-ounce red wine
- 2-ounce whiskey
- 2 tablespoons minced fresh rosemary
- 1 tablespoon minced garlic
- Black pepper
- 6 (1¼-pound) lamb shanks

Directions:

1. In a bowl, add all ingredients except lamb shank and mix till well combined.
2. In a large resealable bag, add marinade and lamb shank.
3. Seal the bag and shake to coat completely.
4. Refrigerate for about 24 hours.
5. Preheat the pallet grill to 225 degrees F.
6. Arrange the leg of lamb in pallet grill and cook for about 4 hours.

Nutrition: Calories: 1507 Cal Fat: 62 g Carbohydrates: 68.7 g Protein:163.3 g Fiber: 6 g

GRILL POULTRY RECIPES

Traeger Chile Lime Chicken

Preparation Time: 2 Minutes

Cooking Time: 15 Minutes

Servings: 1

Ingredients

- 1 chicken breast
- 1 tbsp oil
- 1 tbsp spice ology Chile Lime Seasoning

Directions:

1. Preheat your Traeger to 4000F.
2. Brush the chicken breast with oil then sprinkle the chile-lime seasoning and salt.
3. Place the chicken breast on the grill and cook for 7 minutes on each side or until the internal temperature reaches 1650F.
4. Serve when hot and enjoy.

Nutrition: Calories 131, Total fat 5g, Saturated fat 1g, Total carbs 4g, Net carbs 3g Protein 19g, Sugars 1g, Fiber 1g, Sodium 235mg

Traeger Grilled Buffalo Chicken

Preparation Time: 5 Minutes

Cooking Time: 10 Minutes

Servings: 6

Ingredients

- 5 chicken breasts, boneless and skinless
- 2 tbsp homemade BBQ rub
- 1 cup homemade Cholula Buffalo sauce

Directions:

1. Preheat the Traeger to 4000F.
2. Slice the chicken breast lengthwise into strips. Season the slices with BBQ rub.
3. Place the chicken slices on the grill and paint both sides with buffalo sauce.
4. Cook for 4 minutes with the lid closed. Flip the breasts, paint again with sauce, and cook until the internal temperature reaches 1650F.
5. Remove the chicken from the Traeger and serve when warm.

Nutrition: Calories 176, Total fat 4g, Saturated fat 1g, Total carbs 1g, Net carbs 1g Protein 32g, Sugars 1g, Fiber 0g, Sodium 631mg

Traeger Sheet Pan Chicken Fajitas

Preparation Time: 10 Minutes

Cooking Time: 10 Minutes

Servings: 10

Ingredients

- 2 lb. chicken breast
- 1 onion, sliced
- 1 red bell pepper, seeded and sliced
- 1 orange-red bell pepper, seeded and sliced
- 1 tbsp salt
- 1/2 tbsp onion powder
- 1/2 tbsp granulated garlic
- 2 tbsp Spice ologist Chile Margarita Seasoning
- 2 tbsp oil

Directions:

1. Preheat the Traeger to 4500F and line a baking sheet with parchment paper.
2. In a mixing bowl, combine seasonings and oil then toss with the peppers and chicken.
3. Place the baking sheet in the Traeger and let heat for 10 minutes with the lid closed.
4. Open the lid and place the veggies and the chicken in a single layer. Close the lid and cook for 10 minutes or until the chicken is no longer pink.
5. Serve with warm tortillas and top with your favorite toppings.

Nutrition: Calories 211, Total fat 6g, Saturated fat 1g, Total carbs 5g, Net carbs 4g Protein 29g, Sugars 4g, Fiber 1g, Sodium 360mg

Traeger Asian Miso Chicken wings

Preparation Time: 15 Minutes

Cooking Time: 25 Minutes

Servings: 6

Ingredients

- 2 lb. chicken wings
- 3/4 cup soy
- 1/2 cup pineapple juice
- 1 tbsp sriracha
- 1/8 cup miso
- 1/8 cup gochujang
- 1/2 cup water
- 1/2 cup oil
- Togarashi

Directions:

1. Preheat the Traeger to 3750F
2. Combine all the ingredients except togarashi in a zip lock bag. Toss until the chicken wings are well coated. Refrigerate for 12 hours
3. Pace the wings on the grill grates and close the lid. Cook for 25 minutes or until the internal temperature reaches 1650F
4. Remove the wings from the Traeger and sprinkle Togarashi.
5. Serve when hot and enjoy.

Nutrition: Calories 703, Total fat 56g, Saturated fat 14g, Total carbs 24g, Net carbs 23g Protein 27g, Sugars 6g, Fiber 1g, Sodium 1156mg

Yan's Grilled Quarters

Preparation Time: 20 minutes (additional 2-4 hours marinade)

Cooking Time: 1 to 1.5 hours

Servings: 4

Ingredients:

- 4 fresh or thawed frozen chicken quarters
- 4-6 glasses of extra virgin olive oil
- 4 tablespoons of Yang's original dry lab

Directions:

1. Configure a wood pellet smoker grill for indirect cooking and use the pellets to preheat to 325 ° F.
2. Place chicken on grill and cook at 325 ° F for 1 hour.
3. After one hour, raise the pit temperature to 400 ° F to finish the chicken and crisp the skin.
4. When the inside temperature of the thickest part of the thighs and feet reaches 180 ° F and the juice becomes clear, pull the crispy chicken out of the grill.
5. Let the crispy grilled chicken rest under a loose foil tent for 15 minutes before eating.

Nutrition: Calories 956, Total fat 47g, Saturated fat 13g, Total carbs 1g, Net carbs 1g Protein 124g, Sugars 0g, Fiber 0g, Sodium 1750mg

Cajun Patch Cock Chicken

Preparation Time: 30 minutes (additional 3 hours marinade)

Cooking Time: 2.5 hours

Servings: 4

Ingredients:

- 4-5 pounds of fresh or thawed frozen chicken
- 4-6 glasses of extra virgin olive oil
- Cajun Spice Lab 4 tablespoons or Lucile Bloody Mary Mix Cajun Hot Dry Herb Mix Seasoning

Directions:

1. Use hickory, pecan pellets, or blend to configure a wood pellet smoker grill for indirect cooking and preheat to 225 ° F.
2. If the unit has a temperature meat probe input, such as a MAK Grills 2 Star, insert the probe into the thickest part of the breast.
3. Make chicken for 1.5 hours.
4. After one and a half hours at 225 ° F, raise the pit temperature to 375 ° F and roast until the inside temperature of the thickest part of the chest reaches 170 ° F and the thighs are at least 180 ° F.
6. Place the chicken under a loose foil tent for 15 minutes before carving.

Nutrition: Calories 956, Total fat 47g, Saturated fat 13g, Total carbs 1g, Net carbs 1g Protein 124g, Sugars 0g, Fiber 0g, Sodium 1750mg

TURKEY, RABBIT AND VEAL

Wild Turkey Egg Rolls

Preparation Time: 10 minutes

Cooking Time: 55 minutes

Servings: 1

Ingredients:

- Corn - ½ cup
- Leftover wild turkey meat - 2 cups
- Black beans - ½ cup
- Taco seasoning - 3 tablespoon
- Water ½ cup
- Rotel chilies and tomatoes - 1 can
- Egg roll wrappers- 12
- Cloves of minced garlic- 4
- 1 chopped Poblano pepper or 2 jalapeno peppers
- Chopped white onion - ½ cup

Directions:

1. Add some olive oil to a fairly large skillet. Heat it over medium heat on a stove.
2. Add peppers and onions. Sauté the mixture for 2-3 minutes until it turns soft.
3. Add some garlic and sauté for another 30 seconds. Add the Rotel chilies and beans to the mixture. Keeping mixing the content gently. Reduce the heat and then simmer.
4. After about 4-5 minutes, pour in the taco seasoning and 1/3 cup of water over the meat. Mix everything and coat the meat well. If you feel that it is a bit dry, you can add 2 tablespoons of water. Keep cooking until everything is heated all the way through.
5. Remove the content from the heat and box it to store in a refrigerator. Before you stuff the mixture into the egg wrappers, it should be completely cool to avoid breaking the rolls.
6. Place a spoonful of the cooked mixture in each wrapper and then wrap it securely and tightly. Do the same with all the wrappers.
7. Preheat the traeger grill and brush it with some oil. Cook the egg rolls for 15 minutes on both sides, until the exterior is nice and crispy.
8. Remove them from the grill and enjoy with your favorite salsa!

Nutrition: Carbohydrates: 26.1 g Protein: 9.2 g Fat: 4.2 g Sodium: 373.4 mg Cholesterol: 19.8 mg

Trager Smoked Spatchcock Turkey
Preparation time: 30 minutes

Cooking time: 1 hour 15 minutes

Servings: 8

Ingredients:

- turkey
- 1/2 cup melted butter
- 1/4 cup Traeger chicken rub
- 1 Tablespoon onion powder
- 1 Tablespoon garlic powder
- 1 Tablespoon rubbed sage

Direction:

1. Preheat your Traeger to high temperature.
2. Place the turkey on a chopping board with the breast side down and the legs pointing towards you.
3. Cut either side of the turkey backbone, to remove the spine. Flip the turkey and place it on a pan
4. Season both sides with the seasonings and place it on the grill skin side up on the grill.
5. Cook for 30 minutes, reduce temperature, and cook for 45 more minutes or until the internal temperature reaches 1650F.
6. Remove from the Traeger and let rest for 15 minutes before slicing and serving.

Nutrition: Calories 156, Total fat 16g, Protein 2g, Fiber 0g, Sodium 19mg

Grilled Filet Mignon

Preparation Time: 10 minutes

Cooking Time: 20 minutes

Servings: 1

Ingredients:

- Salt
- Pepper
- Filet mignon - 3

Directions:

1. Preheat your grill to 450 degrees.
2. Season the steak with a good amount of salt and pepper to enhance its flavor.
3. Place on the grill and flip after 5 minutes.
4. Grill both sides for 5 minutes each.
5. Take it out when it looks cooked and serve with your favorite side dish.

Nutrition: Carbohydrates: 0 g Protein: 23 g Fat: 15 g Sodium: 240 mg Cholesterol: 82 mg

Buttery Apple Smoked Turkey

Preparation time: 30 minutes

Cooking Time: 6 Hours

Servings: 1

Ingredients:

- Whole Turkey - 1 (10-lbs., 4.5-kgs)
- The Rub
- Minced garlic – 2 tablespoons
- Salt – 2 ½ tablespoons
- The Filling
- Garlic powder – 1 ½ tablespoons
- Black pepper – 1 ½ tablespoons
- Butter – 1 cup
- Unsweetened apple juice – 1 cup
- Fresh apples – 2
- Chopped onion – 1 cup
- The Fire
- Preheat the smoker an hour prior to smoking.
- Use charcoal and hickory wood chips for smoking.

Directions:

1. Preheat a smoker to 225°F (107°C) with charcoal and hickory wood chips.
2. Rub the turkey with salt and minced garlic then set aside.
3. After that, cut the apples into cubes then combine with garlic powder, black pepper, butter, and chopped onion.
4. Pour the unsweetened apple juice over the filling mixture then mix well.
5. Fill the turkey's cavity with the filling mixture then cover the turkey with aluminum foil.
6. Place in the smoker once the smoker is ready and smoke it for 10 hours or until the internal temperature has reached 180°F (82°C). Don't forget to check the smoke and add more wood chips if it is necessary.
7. When the turkey is done, remove from the smoker then let it sit for a few minutes.
8. Unwrap the turkey then place on a flat surface.
9. Cut the turkey into pieces or slices then serve.
10. Enjoy.

Nutrition: Carbohydrates: 37 g Protein: 9 g Sodium: 565 mg Cholesterol: 49 mg

Smoked Turkey Legs grill

Preparation Time: 30 minutes

Cooking Time: 6 Hours

Servings: 1

Ingredients:

- 4 turkey legs
- 2 bay leaves
- 1 cup of BBQ rubs
- 1 tablespoon of crushed allspice berries
- 2 teaspoons of liquid smoke
- ½ gal of cold water
- 4 cups of ice
- 1 gal of warm water
- ½ cup of brown sugar
- ½ cup of curing salt
- 1 tablespoon of peppercorns; whole black

Directions:

1. Take a large stockpot and mix a gallon of warm water to curing salt, rub, peppercorns, brown sugar, liquid smoke, allspice and bay leaves
2. Bring this mix to boil by keeping the flame on high heat and let all salt granules dissolve thoroughly
3. Now let it cool to room temperature
4. Now add ice and cold water and let the whole thing chill in the refrigerator
5. Add turkey legs and make sure they are submerged in the brine
6. Let it stay for a day
7. Now drain the turkey legs and get rid of the brine
8. Wash off the brine from the legs with the help of cold water and then pat it dry
9. Set the grill to preheat by keeping the temperature to 250 degrees F
10. Lay the legs directly on the grate of the grill
11. Smoke it for 4 to 5 hours till the internal temperature reaches 165 degrees F
12. Serve and enjoy

Nutrition: Carbohydrates: 39 g Protein: 29 g Sodium: 15 mg Cholesterol: 19 mg

Smoked Turkey in Beer Brine

Preparation time: 30 minutes

Cooking Time: 6 Hours

Servings: 1

Ingredients:

- Whole Turkey - 1 (10-lbs., 4.5-kgs)
- The Brine
- Water – 1 liter
- Salt – 2 cups
- Brown sugar – 1 sugar
- Bay leaves – 3 leaves
- Thyme – 1 cup
- Chopped onion – 1 cup
- Cold beer – 1 gallon
- The Fire
- Preheat the smoker an hour prior to smoking.
- Use charcoal and hickory wood chips for smoking.

Directions:

1. Pour water into a pot then add salt, brown sugar, bay leaves, thyme, and chopped onion. Bring to boil.
2. Once it is boiled, remove from heat and let it cool. Usually, it will take approximately 30 minutes.
3. When the brine is cool, transfer to a container then pour cold beer into it. Mix until incorporated.
4. Add turkey to the container then refrigerate for 24 hours until the turkey is completely seasoned.
5. After 24 hours, remove from the refrigerator and dry using a paper towel. Set aside.
6. Preheat a smoker to 225°F (107°C) with charcoal and hickory wood chips.
7. Place the turkey in the sm0ker then smoke for 6 hours or until the internal temperature has reached 160°F (71°C).
8. Remove the smoked turkey from the smoker then let it warm.
9. Cut the smoked turkey into pieces or slices then arrange on a serving dish.
10. Serve and enjoy.

Nutrition: Carbohydrates: 37 g Protein: 9 g Sodium: 565 mg Cholesterol: 49 mg

Hot Smoked Turkey with Jelly Glaze

Preparation time: 30 minutes

Cooking Time: 6 Hours

Servings: 1

Ingredients:

- Whole Turkey - 1 (10-lbs., 4.5-kgs)
- The Rub
- Olive oil – ½ cup
- Salt – 3 tablespoons
- Pepper – 2 tablespoons
- The Glaze
- Hot pepper jelly – ¾ cup
- Rice vinegar – 3 tablespoons
- Red pepper flakes – ¼ cup

The Fire

- Preheat the smoker an hour prior to smoking.
- Use charcoal and hickory wood chips for smoking.

Directions:

1. Preheat a smoker to 225°F (107°C) with charcoal and hickory wood chips. Wait until the smoker is ready.
2. Cut the excess fat of the turkey then brush all sides of the turkey with olive oil,
3. Sprinkle salt and pepper over the turkey then place it in the smoker.
4. Smoke the turkey for 6 hours or until the internal temperature has reached 160°F (71°C).
5. Meanwhile, combine hot pepper jelly with rice vinegar and red pepper flakes then mix well.
6. After 6 hours, brush the smoked turkey with the hot pepper jelly mixture then return to the smoker.
7. Smoke for about 20 minutes then remove from the smoker.
8. Let the smoked turkey warm for a few minutes then cut into slices.
9. Arrange on a serving dish then serve.
10. Enjoy!

Nutrition: Carbohydrates: 27 g Protein: 19 g Sodium: 65 mg Cholesterol: 49 mg

SMOKING RECIPES

Smoked Ribs

Preparation Time: 20 minutes

Cooking Time: 6 hours

Servings: 8

Ingredients:

- Four baby back ribs
- 1 cup pork rubs
- 1 cup barbecue sauce

Directions:

1. Preheat your grill to 180 tiers F for 15 minutes simultaneously as the lid is closed.
2. Sprinkle toddler again ribs with beef rub.
3. Smoke the ribs for 5 hours.
4. Brush the ribs with barbecue sauce.
5. Wrap the ribs with foil.
6. Put the ribs again on the grill.
7. Increase temperature to 350 levels F.
8. Cook for forty-five minutes to at least one hour.
9. Let rest before slicing and serving.

Nutrition: Energy (calories): 493 kcal Protein: 38.78 g Fat: 30.94 g Carbohydrates: 14.97 g

Smoked Pot Roast

Preparation Time: 30 minutes

Cooking Time: 6 hours

Servings: 4

Ingredients:

- Salt and pepper to taste
- 1 tsp. Onion powder 1 tsp. garlic powder
- 3 lb. chuck roast
- 2 cups potatoes, sliced in half
- 2 cups carrots, sliced
- Two onions, peeled
- 1 tsp. chili powder
- 1 cup red wine
- 1 tbsp. fresh rosemary, chopped
- 1 tbsp. fresh thyme, chopped
- Two dried chipotle peppers
- 2 cups beef stock

Directions:

1. Mix the salt, pepper, onion powder, and garlic powder in a bowl.
2. Rub chuck roast with this aggregate.
3. Preheat your pellet grill to 180 ranges F for 15 minutes while the lid is closed.
4. Smoke the pork for 1 hour.
5. Increase temperature to 275 tiers F.
6. Place the pork and the relaxation of the ingredients in a Dutch oven.
7. Seal the Dutch oven and area on the grill.
8. Braise for five hours.

Nutrition: Energy (calories): 733 kcal Protein: 95.53 g Fat: 29.17 g Carbohydrates: 20.59 g

Smoked Brisket

Preparation Time: 30 minutes

Cooking Time: 12 hours

Servings: 8

Ingredients:

- Salt and pepper to taste
- 2 tbsp. beef rub
- 1 tbsp. Worcestershire sauce
- 6 lb. brisket
- 1 cup beef broth

Directions:

1. Mix salt, pepper, beef rub, and Worcestershire sauce in a bowl.
2. Rub brisket with this combination.
3. Preheat your wood pellet grill to 180 levels F for 15 minutes while the lid is closed.
4. Smoke the brisket for 7 hours.
5. Transfer brisket on top of a foil.
6. Pour the broth over the brisket.
7. Wrap it with foil.
8. Smoke for five hours.
9. Let rest before slicing.

Nutrition: Energy (calories): 464 kcal Protein: 73.34 g Fat: 17.43 g Carbohydrates: 3.54 g

Traeger Smoked Potatoes

Preparation Time: 30 minutes

Cooking Time: 1 hour

Servings: 6

Ingredients:

- 2 tbsp. butter
- 1/2 cup milk
- 1 cup heavy cream
- Two cloves garlic, crushed and minced
- 2 tbsp. flour
- Four potatoes, sliced thinly
- Salt and pepper to taste
- 1 cup cheddar cheese, grated

Directions:

1. Preheat your wood pellet grill to 375 levels F for 15 minutes at the same time as the lid is closed.
2. Add butter to your forged iron pan.
3. In a bowl, blend the milk, cream, garlic, and flour.
4. Arrange some of the potatoes in a pan.
5. Season with salt and pepper.
6. Pour some of the sauce over the potatoes.
7. Repeat layers till elements were used.
8. Grill for 50 minutes.
9. Sprinkle cheese on top and prepare dinner for 10 minutes.

Nutrition: Energy (calories): 176 kcal Protein: 2.78 g Fat: 12 g Carbohydrates: 15.14 g

FISH AND SEAFOOD RECIPES

Grilled Lobster Tail

Preparation Time: 10 minutes

Cooking Time: 15 minutes

Servings: 4

Ingredients:

- 2 (8 ounces each) lobster tails
- 1/4 tsp old bay seasoning
- ½ tsp oregano
- 1 tsp paprika
- Juice from one lemon
- 1/4 tsp Himalayan salt
- 1/4 tsp freshly ground black pepper
- 1/4 tsp onion powder
- 2 tbsp freshly chopped parsley
- ¼ cup melted butter

Directions:

1. Slice the tail in the middle with a kitchen shear. Pull the shell apart slightly and run your hand through the meat to separate the meat partially
2. Combine the seasonings
3. Drizzle lobster tail with lemon juice and season generously with the seasoning mixture.
4. Preheat your wood pellet smoker to 450°F, using apple wood pellets.
5. Place the lobster tail directly on the grill grate, meat side down. Cook for about 15 minutes.
6. The tails must be pulled off and it must cool down for a few minutes
7. Drizzle melted butter over the tails.
8. Serve and garnish with fresh chopped parsley.

Nutrition: Calories: 146 Cal Fat: 11.7 g Carbohydrates: 2.1 g   Protein: 9.3 g Fiber: 0.8 g

Halibut

Preparation Time: 10 minutes

Cooking Time: 3o minutes

Servings: 4

Ingredients:

- 1-pound fresh halibut filet (cut into 4 equal sizes)
- 1 tbsp fresh lemon juice
- 2 garlic cloves (minced)
- 2 tsp soy sauce
- ½ tsp ground black pepper
- ½ tsp onion powder
- 2 tbsp honey
- ½ tsp oregano
- 1 tsp dried basil
- 2 tbsp butter (melted)
- Maple syrup for serving

Directions:

1. Combine the lemon juice, honey, soy sauce, onion powder, oregano, dried basil, pepper and garlic.
2. Brush the halibut filets generously with the filet the mixture. Wrap the filets with aluminum foil and refrigerate for 4 hours.
3. Remove the filets from the refrigerator and let them sit for about 2 hours, or until they are at room temperature.
4. Activate your wood pellet grill on smoke, leaving the lid opened for 5 minutes or until fire starts.
5. The lid must not be opened for it to be preheated and reach 275°F 15 minutes, using fruit wood pellets.
6. Place the halibut filets directly on the grill grate and smoke for 30 minutes
7. Remove the filets from the grill and let them rest for 10 minutes.
8. Serve and top with maple syrup to taste

Nutrition: Calories: 180 Cal Fat: 6.3 g Carbohydrates: 10 g Protein: 20.6 g Fiber: 0.3 g

Grilled Salmon

Preparation Time: 10 minutes

Cooking Time: 4o minutes

Servings: 8

Ingredients:

- 2 pounds salmon (cut into fillets)
- 1/2 cup low sodium soy sauce
- 2 garlic cloves (grated)
- 4 tbsp olive oil
- 2 tbsp honey
- 1 tsp ground black pepper
- ½ tsp smoked paprika
- ½ tsp Italian seasoning
- 2 tbsp chopped green onion

Directions:

1. Incorporate pepper, paprika, Italian seasoning, garlic, soy sauce and olive oil. Add the salmon fillets and toss to combine. Cover the bowl and refrigerate for 1 hour.
2. Remove the fillets from the marinade and let it sit for about 2 hours, or until it is at room temperature.
3. Start the wood pellet on smoke, leaving the lid opened for 5 minutes, or until fire starts.
4. Keep lid unopened and preheat grill to a temperature 350°F for 15 minutes.
5. Do not open lid for 4 minutes or until cooked
6. Flip the fillets and cook for additional 25 minutes or until the fish is flaky.
7. Remove the fillets from heat and let it sit for a few minutes.
8. Serve warm and garnish with chopped green onion.

Nutrition: Calories: 317 Cal Fat: 18.8 g Carbohydrates: 8.3 g Protein: 30.6 g Fiber: 0.4 g

Barbeque Shrimp

Preparation Time: 20 minutes

Cooking Time: 8 minutes

Servings: 6

Ingredients:

- 2-pound raw shrimp (peeled and deveined)
- ¼ cup extra virgin olive oil
- ½ tsp paprika
- ½ tsp red pepper flakes
- 2 garlic cloves (minced)
- 1 tsp cumin
- 1 lemon (juiced)
- 1 tsp kosher salt
- 1 tbsp chili paste
- Bamboo or wooden skewers (soaked for 30 minutes, at least)

Directions:

1. Combine the pepper flakes, cumin, lemon, salt, chili, paprika, garlic and olive oil. Add the shrimp and toss to combine.
2. Transfer the shrimp and marinade into a zip-lock bag and refrigerate for 4 hours.
3. Let shrimp rest in room temperature after pulling it out from marinade
4. Start your grill on smoke, leaving the lid opened for 5 minutes, or until fire starts. Use hickory wood pellet.
5. Keep lid unopened and preheat the grill to "high" for 15 minutes.
6. Thread shrimps onto skewers and arrange the skewers on the grill grate.
7. Smoke shrimps for 8 minutes, 4 minutes per side.
8. Serve and enjoy.

Nutrition: Calories: 267 Cal Fat: 11.6 g Carbohydrates: 4.9 g   Protein: 34.9 g Fiber: 0.4 g

Traeger Grilled Tuna steaks

Preparation Time: 5 minutes

Cooking Time: 4 minutes

Servings: 4

Ingredients:

- 4 (6 ounce each) tuna steaks (1 inch thick)
- 1 lemon (juiced)
- 1 clove garlic (minced)
- 1 tsp chili
- 2 tbsp extra virgin olive oil
- 1 cup white wine
- 3 tbsp brown sugar
- 1 tsp rosemary

Directions:

1. Combine lemon, chili, white wine, sugar, rosemary, olive oil and garlic. Add the tuna steaks and toss to combine.
2. Transfer the tuna and marinade to a zip-lock bag. Refrigerate for 3 hours.
3. Remove the tuna steaks from the marinade and let them rest for about 1 hour
4. Start your grill on smoke, leaving the lid opened for 5 minutes, or until fire starts.
5. Do not open lid to preheat until 15 minutes to the setting "HIGH"
6. Grease the grill grate with oil and place the tuna on the grill grate. Grill tuna steaks for 4 minutes, 2 minutes per side.
7. Remove the tuna from the grill and let them rest for a few minutes.

Nutrition: Calories: 137 Cal Fat: 17.8 g Carbohydrates: 10.2 g Protein: 51.2 g Fiber: 0.6 g

Oyster in Shells

Preparation Time: 25 minutes

Cooking Time: 8 minutes

Servings: 4

Ingredients:

- 12 medium oysters
- 1 tsp oregano
- 1 lemon (juiced)
- 1 tsp freshly ground black pepper
- 6 tbsp unsalted butter (melted)
- 1 tsp salt or more to taste
- 2 garlic cloves (minced)
- 2 ½ tbsp grated parmesan cheese
- 2 tbsp freshly chopped parsley

Directions:

1. Remove dirt
2. Open the shell completely. Discard the top shell.
3. Gently run the knife under the oyster to loosen the oyster foot from the bottom shell.
4. Repeat step 2 and 3 for the remaining oysters.
5. Combine melted butter, lemon, pepper, salt, garlic and oregano in a mixing bowl.
6. Pour ½ to 1 tsp of the butter mixture on each oyster.
7. Start your wood pellet grill on smoke, leaving the lid opened for 5 minutes, or until fire starts.
8. Keep lid unopened to preheat in the set "HIGH" with lid closed for 15 minutes.
9. Gently arrange the oysters onto the grill grate.
10. Grill oyster for 6 to 8 minutes or until the oyster juice is bubbling and the oyster is plump.
11. Remove oysters from heat. Serve and top with grated parmesan and chopped parsley.

Nutrition: Calories: 200 Cal Fat: 19.2 g Carbohydrates: 3.9 g Protein: 4.6 g Fiber: 0.8 g

Grilled King Crab Legs

Preparation Time: 10 minutes

Cooking Time: 25 minutes

Servings: 4

Ingredients:

- 4 pounds king crab legs (split)
- 4 tbsp lemon juice
- 2 tbsp garlic powder
- 1 cup butter (melted)
- 2 tsp brown sugar
- 2 tsp paprika
- Black pepper (depends to your liking)

Directions:

1. In a mixing bowl, combine the lemon juice, butter, sugar, garlic, paprika and pepper.
2. Arrange the split crab on a baking sheet, split side up.
3. Drizzle ¾ of the butter mixture over the crab legs.
4. Configure your pellet grill for indirect cooking and preheat it to 225°F, using mesquite wood pellets.
5. Arrange the crab legs onto the grill grate, shell side down.
6. Cover the grill and cook 25 minutes.
7. Remove the crab legs from the grill.
8. Serve and top with the remaining butter mixture.

Nutrition: Calories: 480 Cal Fat: 53.2 g Carbohydrates: 6.1 g Protein: 88.6 g Fiber: 1.2 g

Cajun Smoked Catfish

Preparation Time: 15 minutes

Cooking Time: 2 hours

Servings: 4

Ingredients:

- 4 catfish fillets (5 ounces each)
- ½ cup Cajun seasoning
- 1 tsp ground black pepper
- 1 tbsp smoked paprika
- 1 /4 tsp cayenne pepper
- 1 tsp hot sauce
- 1 tsp granulated garlic
- 1 tsp onion powder
- 1 tsp thyme
- 1 tsp salt or more to taste
- 2 tbsp chopped fresh parsley

Directions:

1. Pour water into the bottom of a square or rectangular dish. Add 4 tbsp salt. Arrange the catfish fillets into the dish. Cover the dish and refrigerate for 3 to 4 hours.
2. Combine the paprika, cayenne, hot sauce, onion, salt, thyme, garlic, pepper and Cajun seasoning in a mixing bowl.
3. Remove the fish from the dish and let it sit for a few minutes, or until it is at room temperature. Pat the fish fillets dry with a paper towel.
4. Rub the seasoning mixture over each fillet generously.
5. Start your grill on smoke, leaving the lid opened for 5 minutes, or until fire starts.
6. Keep lid unopened and preheat to 200°F, using mesquite hardwood pellets.
7. Arrange the fish fillets onto the grill grate and close the grill. Cook for about 2 hours, or until the fish is flaky.
8. Remove the fillets from the grill and let the fillets rest for a few minutes to cool.
9. Serve and garnish with chopped fresh parsley.

Nutrition: Calories: 204 Cal Fat: 11.1 g Carbohydrates: 2.7 g Protein: 22.9 g Fiber: 0.6 g

Smoked Scallops

Preparation Time: 10 minutes

Cooking Time: 15 minutes

Servings: 6

Ingredients:

- 2 pounds sea scallops
- 4 tbsp salted butter
- 2 tbsp lemon juice
- ½ tsp ground black pepper
- 1 garlic clove (minced)
- 1 kosher tsp salt
- 1 tsp freshly chopped tarragon

Directions:

1. Let the scallops dry using paper towels and drizzle all sides with salt and pepper to season
2. Place you're a cast iron pan in your grill and preheat the grill to 400°F with lid closed for 15 minutes.
3. Combine the butter and garlic in hot cast iron pan. Add the scallops and stir. Close grill lid and cook for 8 minutes.
4. Flip the scallops and cook for an additional 7 minutes.
5. Remove the scallop from heat and let it rest for a few minutes.
6. Stir in the chopped tarragon. Serve and top with lemon juice.

Nutrition: Calories: 204 Cal Fat: 8.9 g Carbohydrates: 4 g Protein: 25.6 g Fiber: 0.1 g

Grilled Tilapia

Preparation Time: 10 minutes

Cooking Time: 2o minutes

Servings: 6

Ingredients:

- 2 tsp dried parsley
- ½ tsp garlic powder
- 1 tsp cayenne pepper
- ½ tsp ground black pepper
- ½ tsp thyme
- ½ tsp dried basil
- ½ tsp oregano
- 3 tbsp olive oil
- ½ tsp lemon pepper
- 1 tsp kosher salt
- 1 lemon (juiced)
- 6 tilapia fillets
- 1 ½ tsp creole seafood seasoning

Directions:

1. In a mixing bowl, combine spices
2. Brush the fillets with oil and lemon juice.
3. Liberally, season all sides of the tilapia fillets with the seasoning mix.
4. Preheat your grill to 325°F
5. Place a non-stick BBQ grilling try on the grill and arrange the tilapia fillets onto it.
6. Grill for 15 to 20 minutes
7. Remove fillets and cool down

Nutrition: Calories: 176 Cal Fat: 9.6 g Carbohydrates: 1.5 g Protein: 22.3 g Fiber: 0.5 g

Traeger Salmon with Togarashi

Preparation Time: 5 Minutes

Cooking Time: 20 Minutes

Servings: 3

Ingredients:

- One salmon fillet
- 1/4 cup olive oil
- 1/2 tbsp kosher salt
- 1 tbsp Togarashi seasoning

Directions:

1. Preheat your Traeger to 4000F.
2. Place the salmon on a sheet lined with non-stick foil with the skin side down.
3. Rub the oil into the meat, then sprinkle salt and Togarashi.
4. Place the salmon on the grill and cook for 20 minutes or until the internal temperature reaches 1450F with the lid closed.
5. Remove from the Traeger and serve when hot.

Nutrition: Calories 119Total fat 10g Saturated fat 2g Sodium 720mg

VEGETARIAN RECIPES

Kale Chips

Preparation Time: 30 Minutes

Cooking Time: 20 Minutes

Servings: 4

Ingredients:

- 4 cups kale leaves
- Olive oil
- Salt to taste

Directions:

1. Drizzle kale with oil and sprinkle it with salt.
2. Set the Traeger wood pellet grill to 250 degrees F.
3. Preheat it for 15 minutes while the lid is closed.
4. Add the kale leaves to a baking pan.
5. Place the pan on the grill.
6. Cook the kale for 20 minutes or until crispy.

Nutrition: Calories 118 Total fat 7.6g Total carbs 10.8g Protein 5.4g, Sugars 3.7g Fiber 2.5g, Sodium 3500mg Potassium 536mg

Sweet Potato Fries

Preparation Time: 30 Minutes

Cooking Time: 40 Minutes

Servings: 4

Ingredients:

- Three sweet potatoes, sliced into strips
- Four tablespoons olive oil
- Two tablespoons fresh rosemary, chopped
- Salt and pepper to taste

Directions:

1. Set the Traeger wood pellet grill to 450 degrees F.
2. Preheat it for 10 minutes.
3. Spread the sweet potato strips in the baking pan.
4. Toss in olive oil and sprinkle with rosemary, salt, and pepper.
5. Cook for 15 minutes.
6. Flip and cook for another 15 minutes.
7. Flip and cook for ten more minutes.

Nutrition: Calories 118 Total fat 7.6g Total carbs 10.8g Protein 5.4g Sugars 3.7g Fiber 2.5g, Sodium 3500mg Potassium 536mg

Potato Fries with Chipotle Peppers

Preparation Time: 30 Minutes

Cooking Time: 30 Minutes

Servings: 4

Ingredients:

- Four potatoes, sliced into strips
- Three tablespoons olive oil
- Salt and pepper to taste
- 1 cup mayonnaise
- Two chipotle peppers in adobo sauce
- Two tablespoons lime juice

Directions:

1. Set the Traeger wood pellet grill to high.
2. Preheat it for 15 minutes while the lid is closed.
3. Coat the potato strips with oil.
4. Sprinkle with salt and pepper.
5. Put a baking pan on the grate.
6. Transfer potato strips to the pan.
7. Cook potatoes until crispy.
8. Mix the remaining ingredients.
9. Pulse in a food processor until pureed.
10. Serve potato fries with chipotle dip.

Nutrition: Calories 118 Total fat 7.6g Total carbs 10.8g Protein 5.4g Sugars 3.7g Fiber 2.5g, Sodium 3500mg Potassium 536mg

Traeger Grilled Zucchini

Preparation Time: 30 Minutes

Cooking Time: 10 Minutes

Servings: 4

Ingredients:

- Four zucchinis, sliced into strips
- One tablespoon sherry vinegar
- Two tablespoons olive oil
- Salt and pepper to taste
- Two fresh thyme, chopped

Directions:

1. Place the zucchini strips in a bowl.
2. Mix the remaining fixings and pour them into the zucchini.
3. Coat evenly.
4. Set the Traeger wood pellet grill to 350 degrees F.
5. Preheat for 15 minutes while the lid is closed.
6. Place the zucchini on the grill.
7. Cook for 3 minutes per side.

Nutrition: Calories 118 Total fat 7.6g Total carbs 10.8g Protein 5.4g Sugars 3.7g Fiber 2.5g, Sodium 3500mg Potassium 536mg

Smoked Potato Salad

Preparation Time: 1 Hour and 15 Minutes

Cooking Time: 40 Minutes

Servings: 4

Ingredients:

- 2 lb. potatoes
- Two tablespoons olive oil
- 2 cups mayonnaise
- One tablespoon white wine vinegar
- One tablespoon dry mustard
- 1/2 onion, chopped
- Two celery stalks, chopped
- Salt and pepper to taste

Directions:

1. Coat the potatoes with oil.
2. Smoke the potatoes in the Traeger wood pellet grill at 180 degrees F for 20 minutes.
3. Increase temperature to 450 degrees F and cook for 20 more minutes.
4. Transfer to a bowl and let cool.
5. Peel potatoes.
6. Slice into cubes.
7. Refrigerate for 30 minutes.
8. Stir in the rest of the ingredients.

Nutrition: Calories 118 Total fat 7.6g Total carbs 10.8g Protein 5.4g Sugars 3.7g Fiber 2.5g, Sodium 3500mg Potassium 536mg

Baked Parmesan Mushrooms

Preparation Time: 15 Minutes

Cooking Time: 15 Minutes

Servings: 8

Ingredients:

- Eight mushroom caps
- 1/2 cup Parmesan cheese, grated
- 1/2 teaspoon garlic salt
- 1/4 cup mayonnaise
- Pinch paprika
- Hot sauce

Directions:

1. Place mushroom caps in a baking pan.
2. Mix the remaining ingredients in a bowl.
3. Scoop the mixture onto the mushroom.
4. Place the baking pan on the grill.
5. Cook in the Traeger wood pellet grill at 350 degrees F for 15 minutes while the lid is closed.

Nutrition: Calories 118 Total fat 7.6g Total carbs 10.8g Protein 5.4g Sugars 3.7g Fiber 2.5g, Sodium 3500mg Potassium 536mg

Roasted Spicy Tomatoes

Preparation Time: 30 Minutes

Cooking Time: 1 Hour and 30 Minutes

Servings: 4

Ingredients:

- 2 lb. large tomatoes, sliced in half
- Olive oil
- Two tablespoons garlic, chopped
- Three tablespoons parsley, chopped
- Salt and pepper to taste
- Hot pepper sauce

Directions:

1. Set the temperature to 400 degrees F.
2. Preheat it for 15 minutes while the lid is closed.
3. Add tomatoes to a baking pan.
4. Drizzle with oil and sprinkle with garlic, parsley, salt, and pepper.
5. Roast for 1 hour and 30 minutes.
6. Drizzle with hot pepper sauce and serve.

Nutrition: Calories 118 Total fat 7.6g Total carbs 10.8g Protein 5.4g Sugars 3.7g Fiber 2.5g, Sodium 3500mg Potassium 536mg

VEGAN RECIPES

Wood Pellet Smoked Mushrooms

Preparation Time: 15 minutes,

Cooking Time: 45 minutes.

Servings: 5

Ingredients:

- 4 cup Portobello, whole and cleaned
- 1 tbsp. canola oil
- 1 tbsp. onion powder
- 1 tbsp. granulated garlic
- 1 tbsp. salt
- 1 tbsp. pepper

Directions:

1. Put all the ingredients and mix well.
2. Set the wood pellet temperature to 180°F then place the mushrooms directly on the grill.
3. Smoke the mushrooms for 30 minutes.
4. Increase the temperature to high and cook the mushrooms for a further 15 minutes.
5. Serve and enjoy.

Nutrition: Calories: 1680 Fat: 30g Carbs: 10g Protein: 4g Sodium: 514mg, Potassium: 0mg:

Wood Pellet Grilled Zucchini Squash Spears

Preparation Time: 5 minutes,

Cooking Time: 10 minutes.

Servings: 5

Ingredients:

- 4 zucchinis, cleaned and ends cut
- 2 tbsp. olive oil
- 1 tbsp. sherry vinegar
- 2 thyme leaves pulled
- Salt and pepper to taste

Directions:

1. Cut the zucchini into halves then cut each half thirds.
2. Add the rest of the ingredients in a zip lock bag with the zucchini pieces. Toss to mix well.
3. Preheat the wood pellet temperature to 350°F with the lid closed for 15 minutes.
4. Remove the zucchini from the bag and place them on the grill grate with the cut side down.
5. Cook for 4 minutes until the zucchini are tender
6. Remove from grill and serve with thyme leaves. Enjoy.

Nutrition: Calories: 74 Fat: 5.4g Carbs: 6.1g Protein: 2.6g Sugar: 3.9g Fiber: 2.3g Sodium: 302mg Potassium: 599mg:

RED MEAT RECIPES

Chipotle Honey Smoked Beef Roast

Preparation Time: 10 minutes

Cooking Time: 4 hours 20 minutes

Servings: 10

Ingredients:

- Beef roast (5-lbs., 2.3-kg.)
- The Rub Vegetable oil – 2 tablespoons
- Black pepper – 1 ½ tbsp.
- Salt – 1 ½ tbsp.
- Brown sugar – ¾ tablespoon
- Onion powder – ¾ tablespoon
- Mustard – 1 teaspoon
- Garlic powder – 1 ½ tsp.
- Chipotle powder – 1 ½ tsp.
- The Glaze Honey – ½ cup
- Water – 2 tablespoons
- Minced garlic – 1 ½ tbsp.

The Heat

- Hickory wood pellets

Directions:

1. Place the rub ingredients—vegetable oil, black pepper, salt, brown sugar, onion powder, mustard, garlic powder, and chipotle powder in a bowl, and then mix until combined.
2. Rub the beef roast with the spice mixture, and then set aside. Plug the wood pellet smoker and place the wood pellet inside the hopper.
3. Turn the switch on. Set the "Smoke" setting and prepare the wood pellet smoker for indirect heat.
4. Wait until the smoke is ready and adjust the temperature to 275degrees F (135°C). Once the wood pellet smoker has reached the desired temperature, place the seasoned beef roast directly on the grate inside the wood pellet smoker and smoke for 2 hours.
5. In the meantime, combine honey, water, and minced garlic in a bowl, then stir until incorporated. After 2 hours, take the beef roast out of the wood pellet smoker and place it on a sheet of aluminum foil.
6. Leave the wood pellet smoker on and adjust the temperature to 300degrees F (149°C). Baste the beef roast with the glaze mixture, and then wrap it with the aluminum foil. Return the wrapped beef roast to the wood pellet smoker, then smoke for another 2 hours.

7. Once the smoked beef roast's internal temperature has reached 165degrees F (74°C), remove it from the wood pellet smoker.
8. Let the smoked beef roast rest for about 10 minutes, then unwrap it. Transfer the smoked beef roast to a serving dish, then serve. Enjoy!

Nutrition: Energy (calories): 324 kcal Protein: 27.7 g Fat: 13.23 g Carbohydrates: 26.4 g

Lemon Chili Smoked Beef Brisket

Preparation Time: 10 minutes

Cooking Time: 4 hours 10 minutes

Servings: 10

Ingredients:

- Beef brisket (4.5-lbs., 2-kg.)
- The Rub Lemon juice – 3 tablespoons
- Chili powder – ¼ cup
- Salt – 1 ½ tbsp.
- Garlic powder – 2 tablespoons
- Cayenne – 2 teaspoons
- Pepper – 2 teaspoons

The Heat

- Alder wood pellets

Directions:

1. Combine chili powder with salt, garlic powder, cayenne, and pepper, and then mix well. Rub the beef brisket with lemon juice, and then sprinkle the dry spice mixture over the beef brisket.
2. Plug the wood pellet smoker and fill the hopper with wood pellets. Turn the switch on. Set the "Smoke" setting and prepare the wood pellet smoker for indirect heat.
3. Adjust the wood pellet smoker's temperature to 275degrees F (135°C) and wait until it reaches the desired temperature. Place the seasoned beef brisket directly on the grate in the wood pellet smoker and smoke for approximately 3 hours or until the internal temperature has reached 125degrees F (52°C).
4. After 2 hours, take the beef brisket out of the wood pellet smoker and transfer it to a sheet of aluminum foil. Wrap the beef brisket with the aluminum foil, and then return it to the wood pellet smoker.
5. Smoke the wrapped beef brisket for another 2 hours or until the internal temperature has reached 165degrees F (74°C). Once it is done, remove the wrapped smoked beef brisket from the wood pellet smoker and let it rest for about 10 minutes.
6. Unwrap the smoked beef brisket, and then cut into slices.
7. Serve and enjoy.

Nutrition: Energy (calories): 425 kcal Protein: 30.96 g Fat: 30.98 g Carbohydrates: 4.66 g

BAKING RECIPES

Quick Yeast Dinner Rolls

Preparation Time: 5 minutes

Cooking Time: 30 minutes

Servings 8

Ingredients:

- 2 tablespoons yeast, quick rise
- 1 cup water, lukewarm
- 3 cups flour
- ¼ cup sugar
- 1 teaspoon salt
- ¼ cup unsalted butter, softened
- 1 egg
- Cooking spray, as needed
- 1 egg, for egg wash

Directions:

1. Combine the yeast and warm water in a small bowl to activate the yeast. Let sit for about 5 to 10 minutes, or until foamy.
2. Combine the flour, sugar, and salt in the bowl of a stand mixer fitted with the dough hook. Pour the water and yeast into the dry ingredients with the machine running on low speed.
3. Add the butter and egg and mix for 10 minutes, gradually increasing the speed from low to high.
4. Form the dough into a ball and place in a buttered bowl. Cover with a cloth and let the dough rise for approximately 40 minutes.
5. Transfer the risen dough to a lightly floured work surface and divide into 8 pieces, forming a ball with each.
6. Lightly spritz a cast iron pan with cooking spray and arrange the balls in the pan. Cover with a cloth and let rise for 20 minutes.
7. When ready to cook, set Traeger temperature to 375 F (191 C) and preheat, lid closed for 15 minutes.
8. Brush the rolls with the egg wash. Place the pan on the grill and bake for 30 minutes, or until lightly browned.
9. Remove from the grill. Serve hot.

Baked Cornbread with Honey Butter

Preparation Time: 10 minutes

Cooking Time: 35 to 45 minutes

Servings 6

Ingredients:

- 4 ears whole corn
- 1 cup all-purpose flour
- 1 cup cornmeal
- 2/3 cup white sugar
- 1½ teaspoons baking powder
- ½ teaspoon baking soda
- ½ teaspoon salt
- 1 cup buttermilk
- ½ cup butter, softened
- 2 eggs
- ½ cup butter, softened
- ¼ cup honey

Directions:

1. When ready to cook, set Traeger temperature to High and preheat, lid closed for 15 minutes.
2. Peel back the outer layer of the corn husk, keeping it attached to the cob. Remove the silk from the corn and place the husk back into place. Soak the corn in cold water for 10 minutes.
3. Place the corn directly on the grill grate and cook for 15 to 20 minutes, or until the kernels are tender, stirring occasionally. Remove from the grill and set aside.
4. In a large bowl, stir together the flour, cornmeal, sugar, baking powder, baking soda and salt.
5. In a separate bowl, whisk together the buttermilk, butter, and eggs. Pour the wet mixture into the cornmeal mixture and fold together until there are no dry spots. Pour the batter into a greased baking dish.
6. Cut the kernels from the corn and sprinkle over the top of the batter, pressing the kernels down with a spoon to submerge.
7. Turn Traeger temperature down to 350 F (177 C). Place the baking dish on the grill. Bake for about 20 to 25 minutes, or until the top is golden brown and a toothpick inserted into the middle of the cornbread comes out clean.
8. Remove the cornbread from the grill and let cool for 10 minutes before serving.
9. To make the honey butter, mix the butter and honey until combined. Serve the cornbread with the honey butter.

S'mores Dip with Candied Pecans

Preparation Time: 10 minutes

Cooking Time: 37 to 45 minutes

Servings 4

Ingredients:

Candied Smoked Pecans:

- ½ cup sugar
- ½ cup brown sugar
- 1 tablespoon ground cinnamon
- 1 teaspoon salt
- ¼ teaspoon cayenne pepper
- 1 egg white
- 1 teaspoon water
- 1-pound (454 g) pecans

S'mores Dip:

- 1 tablespoon butter
- 2 cups milk chocolate chips
- 10 large marshmallows, cut in half
- Graham crackers, for serving

Directions:

1. When ready to cook, set Traeger temperature to 300 F (149 C) and preheat, lid closed for 15 minutes.
2. In a small bowl, stir together the sugars, cinnamon, salt, and cayenne pepper. In a medium bowl, whisk together the egg white and water until frothy.
3. Pour the pecans into a large bowl. Pour in the egg white mixture and sugar mixture and toss to coat well.
4. Spread the coated pecans on a sheet tray lined with parchment paper. Place the tray directly on the grill grate. Smoke for 30 to 35 minutes, stirring often.
5. Remove from the grill and let cool. Break apart and roughly chop. Set aside.
6. When ready to cook, set Traeger temperature to 400 F (204 C) and preheat, lid closed for 15 minutes.
7. Place a cast iron skillet directly on the grill grate while the grill heats up.
8. When the cast iron skillet is hot, melt the butter in the skillet and swirl around the skillet to coat.
9. Add the chocolate chips to the skillet, then top with the marshmallows. Cook for 7 to 10 minutes, or until the chocolate is melted and marshmallows are lightly browned. Remove from the grill.

Spread a handful of the candied pecans over the

CHEESE AND BREAD

Traeger-Grill Flatbread Pizza

Preparation Time: 10 minutes

Cooking Time: 20 minutes

Servings: 3

Ingredients

Dough

- 2 cups flour
- 1 tbsp salt
- 1 tbsp sugar
- 2 tbsp yeast
- 6 oz warm water

Toppings

- Green/red bell pepper
- 1/2 garlic
- zucchini
- 1/2 onion
- Olive oil
- 5 bacon strips
- 1 cup halved yellow cherry tomatoes
- Sliced jalapenos
- Sliced green olives
- Sliced kalamata olives
- Goat cheese
- For drizzling: Balsamic vinegar

Directions:

1. Combine all dough ingredients in a stand mixer bowl. Mix until the dough is smooth and elastic. Divide into 3 equal balls. Roll each dough ball with a rolling pin into a thin round enough to fit a 12-inch skillet.

2. Grease the skillet using olive oil.
3. Meanwhile, turn your traeger grill on smoke for about 4-5 minutes with the lid open. Turn to high and preheat for about 10-15 minutes with the lid closed.
4. Once ready, arrange peppers, garlic, zucchini, and onion on the grill grate then drizzle with oil and salt. Check at 10 minutes.
5. Now remove zucchini from the grill and add bacon. Continue to cook for another 10 minutes until bacon is done.
6. Transfer the toppings on a chopping board to cool. Chop tomatoes, jalapenos and olive.
7. Brush your crust with oil and smash garlic with a fork over the crust. Smear carefully not to tear the crust.
8. Add toppings to the crust in the skillet.
9. Place the skillet on the grill and cook for about 20 minutes until brown edges.
10. Repeat for the other crusts.
11. Now drizzle each with vinegar and slice.
12. Serve and enjoy.

Nutrition: Calories 342, Total fat 1.2g, Saturated fat 0.2g, Total carbs 70.7g, Net carbs 66.8g, Protein 11.7g, Sugars 4.2g, Fiber 3.9g, Sodium 2333mg, Potassium 250mg

Traeger Smoked Nut Mix

Preparation Time: 15 minutes

Cooking Time: 20 minutes

Servings: 8

Ingredients

- 3 cups mixed nuts (pecans, peanuts, almonds etc.)
- 1/2 tbsp brown sugar
- 1 tbsp thyme, dried
- 1/4 tbsp mustard powder
- 1 tbsp olive oil, extra-virgin

Directions:

1. Preheat your traeger grill to 250oF with the lid closed for about 15 minutes.
2. Combine all ingredients in a bowl, large, then transfer into a cookie sheet lined with parchment paper.
3. Place the cookie sheet on a grill and grill for about 20 minutes.
4. Remove the nuts from the grill and let cool.
5. Serve and enjoy.

Nutrition: Calories 249, Total fat 21.5g, Saturated fat 3.5g, Total carbs 12.3g, Net carbs 10.1g, Protein 5.7g, Sugars 5.6g, Fiber 2.1g, Sodium 111mg, Potassium 205mg

APPETIZERS AND SIDES

Atomic Buffalo Turds

Preparation Time: 30 to 45 Minutes

Cooking Time: 1.5 Hours to 2 Hours   .

Servings: 6

Ingredients:

- 10 Medium Jalapeno Pepper
- 8 ounces regular cream cheese at room temperature
- ¾Cup Monterey Jack and Cheddar Cheese Blend Shred (optional)
- One teaspoon smoked paprika
- One teaspoon garlic powder
- ½ teaspoon cayenne pepper
- Teaspoon red pepper flakes (optional)
- 20 smoky sausages
- Ten sliced bacon, cut in half

Directions:

1. Wear food service gloves when using. Jalapeno peppers are washed vertically and sliced. Carefully remove seeds and veins using a spoon or paring knife and discard. Place Jalapeno on a grilled vegetable tray and set aside.
2. A small bowl, mix cream cheese, shredded cheese, paprika, garlic powder, cayenne pepper is used, and red pepper flakes if used until thoroughly mixed.
3. Mix cream cheese with half of the jalapeno pepper.
4. Place the Little Smokiness sausage on half of the filled jalapeno pepper.
5. Wrap half of the thin bacon around half of each jalapeno peppers.
6. Fix the bacon to the sausage with a toothpick so that the pepper does not pierce. Place the ABT on the grill tray or pan.
7. Set the wood pellet smoker and grill for indirect cooking and preheat to 250 degrees Fahrenheit using hickory pellets or blends.
8. Suck jalapeno peppers at 250 ° F for about 1.5 to 2 hours until the bacon is cooked and crisp.
9. Remove the ABT from the grill and let it rest for 5 minutes before hors d'oeuvres.

Nutrition: Calories: 131 Carbs: 1g Fat: 12g Protein: 5g

Grilled Corn

Preparation Time: 15 minutes

Cooking Time: 25 minutes

Servings: 6

Ingredients:

- Six fresh ears of corn
- Salt
- Black pepper
- Olive oil
- Vegetable seasoning
- Butter for serving

Directions:

1. Preheat the grill to high with a closed lid.
2. Peel the husks. Remove the corn's silk. Rub with black pepper, salt, vegetable seasoning, and oil.
3. Close the husks and grill for 25 minutes. Turn them occasionally.
4. Serve topped with butter and enjoy.

Nutrition: Calories: 70 Protein: 3g Carbs: 18g Fat: 2g

Thyme - Rosemary Mash Potatoes

Preparation Time: 20 minutes

Cooking Time: 1 hour

Servings: 6

Ingredients:

- 4 ½ lbs. Potatoes, russet
- Salt
- 1 pint of Heavy cream
- 3 Thyme sprigs + 2 tablespoons for garnish
- 2 Rosemary sprigs
- 6 - 7 Sage leaves
- 6 - 7 Black peppercorns
- Black pepper to taste
- Two stick Butter softened
- 2 Garlic cloves, chopped

Directions:

1. Preheat the grill to 350F with a closed lid.
2. Peel the russet potatoes.
3. Cut into small pieces and place them in a baking dish. Fill it with water (1 ½ cups). Place on the grill and cook with a closed lid for about 1 hour.
4. In the meantime, in a saucepan, combine the garlic, peppercorns, herbs, and cream. Place on the grate and cook covered for about 15 minutes. Once done, strain to remove the garlic and herbs. Keep warm.
5. Take out the water of the potatoes and place them in a stockpot. Rice them with a fork and pour 2/3 of the mixture. Add one stick of softened butter and salt.
6. Serve right away.

Nutrition: Calories: 180 Protein: 4g Carbs: 28g Fat: 10g

MORE SIDES

<u>Grilled Mushroom Skewers</u>

Preparation Time: 5 Minutes

Cooking Time: 60 Minutes

Servings: 6

Ingredients:

- 16 - oz 1 lb. Baby Portobello Mushrooms

For the marinade:

- ¼ - cup olive oil
- ¼ - cup lemon juice
- Small handful of parsley
- 1 - tsp sugar
- 1 - tsp salt
- ¼ - tsp pepper
- ¼ - tsp cayenne pepper
- 1 to 2 - garlic cloves
- 1 - Tbsp balsamic vinegar

What you will need:

- 10 - inch bamboo/wood skewers

Directions:

1. Add the beans to the plate of a lipped container, in an even layer. Shower the softened spread uniformly out ludicrous, and utilizing a couple of tongs tenderly hurl the beans with the margarine until all around covered.
2. Season the beans uniformly, and generously, with salt and pepper.
3. Preheat the smoker to 275 degrees. Include the beans, and smoke 3-4 hours, hurling them like clockwork or until delicate wilted, and marginally seared in spots.
4. Spot 10 medium sticks into a heating dish and spread with water. It's critical to douse the sticks for in any event 15 minutes (more is better) or they will consume too rapidly on the flame broil.
5. Spot the majority of the marinade fixings in a nourishment processor and heartbeat a few times until marinade is almost smooth.
6. Flush your mushrooms and pat dry. Cut each mushroom down the middle, so each piece has half of the mushroom stem.
7. Spot the mushroom parts into an enormous gallon-size Ziploc sack, or a medium bowl and pour in the marinade. Shake the pack until the majority of the mushrooms are equally covered in marinade. Refrigerate and marinate for 30mins to 45mins.
8. Preheat your barbecue about 300F

9. Stick the mushrooms cozily onto the bamboo/wooden sticks that have been dousing (no compelling reason to dry the sticks). Piercing the mushrooms was a bit of irritating from the outset until I got the hang of things.
10. I've discovered that it's least demanding to stick them by bending them onto the stick. In the event that you simply drive the stick through, it might make the mushroom break.
11. Spot the pierced mushrooms on the hot barbecue for around 3mins for every side, causing sure the mushrooms don't consume to the flame broil. The mushrooms are done when they are delicate; as mushrooms ought to be Remove from the barbecue. Spread with foil to keep them warm until prepared to serve

Nutrition: Calories: 230 Carbs: 10g Fat: 20g Protein: 5g

Caprese Tomato Salad

Preparation Time: 5 Minutes

Cooking Time: 60 Minutes

Servings: 4

Ingredients:

- 3 - cups halved multicolored cherry tomatoes
- 1/8 - teaspoon kosher salt
- ½ - cup fresh basil leaves
- 1 - tablespoon extra-virgin olive oil
- 1 - tablespoon balsamic vinegar
- ½ - teaspoon black pepper
- ¼ - teaspoon kosher salt
- 1 - ounce diced fresh mozzarella cheese (about 1/3 cup)

Directions:

1. Join tomatoes and 1/8 tsp. legitimate salt in an enormous bowl. Let represent 5mins. Include basil leaves, olive oil, balsamic vinegar, pepper, 1/4 tsp. fit salt, and mozzarella; toss.

Nutrition: Calories 80 Fat 5.8g Protein 2g Carb 5g Sugars 4g

Watermelon-Cucumber Salad

Preparation Time: 12 Minutes

Cooking Time: 0 Minutes

Servings: 4

Ingredients:

- 1 - tablespoon olive oil
- 2 - teaspoons fresh lemon juice
- ¼ - teaspoon salt
- 2 - cups cubed seedless watermelon
- 1 - cup thinly sliced English cucumber
- ¼ - cup thinly vertically sliced red onion
- 1 - tablespoon thinly sliced fresh basil

Directions:

1. Consolidate oil, squeeze, and salt in a huge bowl, mixing great. Include watermelon, cucumber, and onion; toss well to coat. Sprinkle plate of mixed greens equally with basil.

Nutrition: Calories 60 Fat 3.5g Protein 0.8g Carb 7.6g

SNACKS

Corn Salsa

Preparation Time: 10 Minutes

Cooking Time: 15 Minutes

Servings: 4

Ingredients:

- 4 Ears Corn, large with the husk on
- 4 Tomatoes (Roma) diced and seeded
- 1 tsp. of Onion powder
- 1 tsp. of Garlic powder
- 1 Onion, diced
- ½ cup chopped Cilantro
- Black pepper and salt to taste
- 1 lime, the juice
- 1 grille jalapeno, diced

Directions:

1. Preheat the grill to 450F.
2. Place the ears corn on the grate and cook until charred. Remove husk. Cut into kernels.
3. Combine all ingredients, plus the corn and mix well. Refrigerate before serving.
4. Enjoy!

Nutrition: Calories: 120 Protein: 2f Carbs: 4g Fat: 1g

Nut Mix on the Grill

Preparation Time: 15 Minutes

Cooking Time: 20 Minutes

Servings: 8

Ingredients:

- 3 cups Mixed Nuts, salted
- 1 tsp. Thyme, dried
- 1 ½ tbsp. brown sugar, packed
- 1 tbsp. Olive oil
- ¼ tsp. of Mustard powder
- ¼ tsp. Cayenne pepper

Directions:

1. Preheat the grill to 250F with closed lid.
2. In a bowl combine the ingredients and place the nuts on a baking tray lined with parchment paper. Place the try on the grill. Cook 20 minutes.
3. Serve and enjoy!

Nutrition: Calories: 65 Protein: 23g Carbs 4g: Fat: 52g

DESSERT RECIPE

Grilled Pineapple with Chocolate Sauce

Preparation Time: 10 Minutes

Cooking Time: 25 Minutes

Servings: 8

Ingredients:

- 1pineapple
- 8 oz bittersweet chocolate chips
- 1/2 cup spiced rum
- 1/2 cup whipping cream
- 2tbsp light brown sugar

Directions:

1. Preheat pellet grill to 400°F.
2. De-skin, the pineapple, then slice the pineapple into 1 in cubes.
3. In a saucepan, combine chocolate chips. When chips begin to melt, add rum to the saucepan. Continue to stir until combined, then add a splash of the pineapple's juice.
4. Add in whipping cream and continue to stir the mixture. Once the sauce is smooth and thickening, lower heat to simmer to keep warm.
5. Thread pineapple cubes onto skewers. Sprinkle skewers with brown sugar.
6. Place skewers on the grill grate. Grill for about 5 minutes per side, or until grill marks begin to develop.
7. Remove skewers from grill and allow to rest on a plate for about 5 minutes. Serve alongside warm chocolate sauce for dipping.

Nutrition: Calories: 112.6 Fat: 0.5 g Cholesterol: 0 Carbohydrate: 28.8 g Fiber: 1.6 g Sugar: 0.1 g Protein: 0.4 g

Nectarine and Nutella Sundae

Preparation Time: 10 Minutes

Cooking Time: 25 Minutes

Servings: 4

Ingredients:

- 2nectarines halved and pitted
- 2tsp honey
- 4tbsp Nutella
- 4scoops vanilla ice cream
- 1/4 cup pecans, chopped
- Whipped cream, to top
- 4cherries, to top

Directions:

1. Preheat pellet grill to 400°F.
2. Slice nectarines in half and remove the pits.
3. Brush the inside (cut side) of each nectarine half with honey.
4. Place nectarines directly on the grill grate, cut side down—Cook for 5-6 minutes, or until grill marks develop.
5. Flip nectarines and cook on the other side for about 2 minutes.
6. Remove nectarines from the grill and allow it to cool.
7. Fill the pit cavity on each nectarine half with 1 tbsp Nutella.
8. Place one scoop of ice cream on top of Nutella. Top with whipped cream, cherries, and sprinkle chopped pecans. Serve and enjoy!

Nutrition: Calories: 90 Fat: 3 g Carbohydrate: 15g Sugar: 13 g Protein: 2 g

Cinnamon Sugar Donut Holes

Preparation Time: 10 Minutes

Cooking Time: 35 Minutes

Servings: 4

Ingredients:

- 1/2 cup flour
- 1tbsp cornstarch
- 1/2 tsp baking powder
- 1/8 tsp baking soda
- 1/8 tsp ground cinnamon
- 1/2 tsp kosher salt
- 1/4 cup buttermilk
- 1/4 cup sugar
- 11/2 tbsp butter, melted
- 1egg
- 1/2 tsp vanilla
- Topping
- 2tbsp sugar
- 1tbsp sugar
- 1tsp ground cinnamon

Directions:

1. Preheat pellet grill to 350°F.
2. In a medium bowl, combine flour, cornstarch, baking powder, baking soda, ground cinnamon, and kosher salt. Whisk to combine.
3. In a separate bowl, combine buttermilk, sugar, melted butter, egg, and vanilla. Whisk until the egg is thoroughly combined.
4. Pour wet mixture into the flour mixture and stir. Stir just until combined, careful not to overwork the mixture.
5. Spray mini muffin tin with cooking spray.
6. Spoon 1 tbsp of donut mixture into each mini muffin hole.
7. Place the tin on the pellet grill grate and bake for about 18 minutes, or until a toothpick can come out clean.
8. Remove muffin tin from the grill and let rest for about 5 minutes.
9. In a small bowl, combine 1 tbsp sugar and 1 tsp ground cinnamon.
10. Melt 2 tbsp of butter in a glass dish. Dip each donut hole in the melted butter, then mix and toss with cinnamon sugar. Place completed donut holes on a plate to serve.

Nutrition: Calories: 190 Fat: 17 g Carbohydrate: 21 g Fiber: 1 g Sugar: 8 g Protein: 3 g

SAUCES AND RUBS

Heavenly Rabbit Smoke

Preparation Time: 10 minutes

Cooking Time: Nil

Serving: 5

Ingredients

- 1 teaspoon dried thyme
- 1 teaspoon dried parsley
- 2 teaspoons dried oregano
- ½ teaspoon dried marjoram
- ½ teaspoon ground nutmeg
- ½ teaspoon ground cinnamon
- 1 teaspoon chicken bouillon granules
- 1 and ½ teaspoons garlic powder
- 1 teaspoon cracked pepper
- ½ teaspoon salt
- 1 and ½ teaspoon onion powder

Directions:

1. Mix the ingredients mentioned above to prepare the seasoning and use it as needed.

Nutrition: Calories: 20 Carbs: 5g Protein: 1g

Uncle Johnny's Rub

Preparation Time: 10 minutes

Cooking Time: Nil

Serving: 4

Ingredients

- ½ teaspoon oregano
- 4 tablespoons ground paprika
- 1 tablespoon brown sugar
- 1 tablespoon ground cumin
- 1 tablespoon chili powder
- 1 tablespoon mustard powder
- 1 tablespoon salt
- 2 tablespoons pepper
- 1 tablespoon garlic powder

Directions:

1. Mix the ingredients mentioned above to prepare the seasoning and use it as needed.

Nutrition: Calories: 20 Carbs: 5g Protein: 1g

Fajita Seasoning

Preparation Time: 10 minutes

Cooking Time: Nil

Serving: 4

Ingredients

- ¼ cup of chili powder
- 2 tablespoon of ground cumin
- 1 tablespoon of salt
- 4 teaspoons of black pepper
- 3 teaspoons of dried oregano
- 2 teaspoons of paprika
- 1 teaspoon of onion powder
- 1 teaspoon of parsley

Directions:

1. Mix the ingredients mentioned above to prepare the seasoning and use it as needed.

Nutrition: Calories: 20 Carbs: 5g Protein: 1g

NUT AND FRUIT RECIPES

Smoked Bananas Foster Bread Pudding

Preparation Time: 1 hour

Cooking Time: 2 hours 15 minutes

Servings: 8 to 10

Ingredients:

- 1loaf (about 4 cups) brioche or challah, cubed into 1-inch cubes
- 3eggs, lightly beaten
- 2cups of milk
- 2/3 cups sugar
- 2large bananas, peeled and smashed
- 1tbsp vanilla extract
- 1tbsp cinnamon
- 1/4 tsp. nutmeg
- 1/2 cup pecans
- Rum Sauce Ingredients:
- 1/2 cup spiced rum
- 1/4 cup unsalted butter
- 1cup dark brown sugar
- 1tsp cinnamon
- 5large bananas, peeled and quartered

Directions:

1. Place pecans on a skillet over medium heat and lightly toast for about 5 minutes, until you can smell them.
2. Remove from heat and allow cooling. Once cooled, chop pecans.
3. Lightly butter a 9" x 13" baking dish and evenly layer bread cubes in the container.
4. In a large bowl, whisk eggs, milk, sugar, mashed bananas, vanilla extract, cinnamon, and nutmeg.
5. Whip the egg mixture over the bread in the baking dish evenly. Sprinkle with chopped pecans. Cover with aluminum foil and refrigerate for about 30 minutes.
6. Preheat pellet grill to 180degrees F. Turn your smoke setting to high, if applicable.
7. Remove foil from dish and place on the smoker for 5 minutes with the lid closed, allowing bread to absorb smoky flavor.
8. Remove the dish from the grill and cover with foil again. Increase your pellet grill's temperature to 350degrees F.
9. Place dish on the grill grate and cook for 50-60 minutes until everything is cooked through and the bread pudding is bubbling.
10. In a saucepan, while pudding cooks, heat butter for rum sauce over medium heat. If the butter begins to melt, add the brown sugar, cinnamon, and bananas. Sauté until bananas start to soften.

11. Add rum and watch. When the liquid begins to bubble, light a match, and tilt the pan. Slowly and carefully move the game towards the fluid until the sauce lights. When the flames go away, remove the skillet from heat.
12. If you're uncomfortable lighting the liquid with a match, just cook it for 3-4 minutes over medium heat after the rum has been added.
13. Keep rum sauce on a simmer or reheat once it's time to serve.
14. Remove bread pudding from the grill and allow it to cool for about 5 minutes.
15. Cut into squares, put each square on a plate, add a banana piece, and then drizzle rum sauce over the top. Serve on its own or a la mode and enjoy it!

Nutrition: Calories: 274.7 Fat: 7.9 g Cholesterol: 10 mg Carbohydrate: 35.5 g Fiber: 0.9 g Sugar: 24.7 g Protein: 4 g

TRADITIONAL RECIPES

Sweet & Spicy Chicken Thighs

Preparation Time: 15 minutes

Cooking Time: 15 minutes

Servings: 4

Ingredients:

- 2 garlic cloves, minced
- ¼ cup honey
- 2 tablespoons soy sauce
- ¼ teaspoon red pepper flakes, crushed
- 4 (5-ounce) skinless, boneless chicken thighs
- 2 tablespoons olive oil
- 2 teaspoons sweet rub
- ¼ teaspoon red chili powder
- Ground black pepper, as required

Directions

1. Preheat the Traeger grill & Smoker on grill setting to 400 degrees F.
2. In a small bowl, add garlic, honey, soy sauce and red pepper flakes and with a wire whisk, beat until well combined.
3. Coat chicken thighs with oil and season with sweet rub, chili powder and black pepper generously.
4. Arrange the chicken drumsticks onto the grill and cook for about 15 minutes per
5. In the last 4-5 minutes of cooking, coat drumsticks with garlic mixture.
6. Serve immediately.

Nutrition: Calories 309 Total Fat 12.1 g Saturated Fat 2.9 g Cholesterol 82 mg Sodium 504 mg Total Carbs 18.7 g Fiber 0.2 g Sugar 17.6 g Protein 32.3 g

SAUCES, RUBS, AND MARINATES

Classic Kansas City BBQ Sauce

Preparation Time: 10 Minutes

Cooking Time: 15 Minutes

Servings: 24

Ingredients:

- 1/4 cup yellow onion, finely chopped
- 2 tablespoons water
- 2 tablespoons vegetable oil
- 2 cups ketchup
- 1/3 cup brown sugar
- 3 cloves garlic, finely chopped
- 1 tablespoon apple cider vinegar
- 1 tablespoon tomato paste
- 1 tablespoon Worcestershire sauce
- 1 teaspoon liquid hickory smoke
- 1 teaspoon ground mustard

Directions:

1. Place the onion in a food processor and pulse until pureed. Add the water to the onion and pulse few more times.
2. In a medium saucepan, heat the oil and add the onion. When the onion is just starting to soften, add the remaining ingredients and stir well.
3. Stretch or roll dough to a 12-inch circle.
4. Cook the sauce at a simmer for fifteen minutes, stirring occasionally.
5. Remove the pan from the heat and allow to cool for thirty minutes before using or storing in a mason jar.

Nutrition: Calories: 799 Sodium: 595mg Dietary Fiber: 8.6g Fat: 52.7g Carbs: 74.9g Protein: 10g

RUBS, INJECTABLES, MARINADES, AND MOPS

Not-Just-For-Pork Rub

Preparation Time: 10 Minutes

Cooking Time: 0 Minutes

Servings: ¼ Cup

Ingredients:

- ½ teaspoon ground thyme
- ½ teaspoon paprika
- ½ teaspoon course kosher salt
- ½ teaspoon garlic powder
- ½ teaspoon onion powder
- ½ teaspoon chili powder
- ¼ teaspoon dried oregano leaves
- ¼ teaspoon freshly ground black pepper
- ¼ teaspoon ground chipotle chile pepper
- ¼ teaspoon celery seed

Directions:

1. In a small airtight container or zip-top bag, combine the thyme, paprika, salt, garlic powder, onion powder, chili powder, oregano, black pepper, chipotle pepper, and celery seed. Close the container and shake to mix. Unused rub will keep in an airtight container for months.

Nutrition: Calories: 20 Carbs: 5g Protein: 1g

Chicken Rub

Preparation Time: 10 Minutes

Cooking Time: 0 Minutes

Servings: ¼ Cup

Ingredients:

- 2 tablespoons packed light brown sugar
- 1½ teaspoons course kosher salt
- 1¼ teaspoons garlic powder
- ½ teaspoon onion powder
- ½ teaspoon freshly ground black pepper
- ½ teaspoon ground chipotle chile pepper
- ½ teaspoon smoked paprika
- ¼ teaspoon dried oregano leaves
- ¼ teaspoon mustard powder
- ¼ teaspoon cayenne pepper

Directions:

1. In a small airtight container or zip-top bag, combine the brown sugar, salt, garlic powder, onion powder, black pepper, chipotle pepper, paprika, oregano, mustard, and cayenne. Close the container and shake to mix. Unused rub will keep in an airtight container for months.

Nutrition: Calories: 20 Carbs: 5g Protein: 1g

OTHER RECIPES YOU NEVER THOUGHT ABOUT TO GRILL

Summer Treat Corn

Preparation time: 10 minutes

Cooking time 20 minutes

Servings: 6

Ingredients

- 6 fresh whole corn on the cob
- One-half C. butter
- Salt

Direction

1. Set the temperature of Traeger Grill to 400 degrees F and preheat with closed lid for 15 mins.
2. Husk the corn and remove all the silk.
3. Brush each corn with melted butter and sprinkle with salt.
4. Place the corn onto the grill and cook for about 20 mins, rotating after every 5 mins and brushing with butter once halfway through.
5. Serve warm.

Nutrition: Energy (calories): 1196 kcal Protein: 30.76 g Fat: 38.84 g Carbohydrates: 218.81 g Calcium, Ca35 mg Magnesium, Mg280 mg Phosphorus, P745 mg Iron, Fe6 mg

Crunchy Potato Wedges

Preparation time: 15 minutes

Cooking time 16minutes

Servings: 5

Ingredients

- 4 Yukon gold potatoes
- 2 tbsp. olive oil
- 1 tbsp. garlic, minced
- 2 tsp. onion powder
- One-half tsp. red pepper flakes, crushed
- Salt and freshly ground black pepper, to taste

Direction

1. Keep the oven of the Traeger Grill to 400 degrees F and heat it up it for 15 minutes with the cover closed.
2. Cut each potato into 8 equal-sized wedges.
3. In a large bowl, add potato wedges and remaining ingredients and toss to coat well.
4. Arrange the potato wedges onto the grill and cook for about 8 mins per side.
5. Remove from grill and serve hot.

Nutrition: Energy (calories): 353 kcal Protein: 7.83 g Fat: 7.12 g Carbohydrates: 66.65 g Calcium, Ca54 mg Magnesium, Mg88 mg Phosphorus, P220 m Iron, Fe3.07 mg

Twice Grilled Potatoes

Preparation time: 20 minutes

Cooking time 4 hours

Servings: 4

Ingredients

- 6 russet potatoes
- 2 tbsp. olive oil
- Salt
- 8 cooked bacon slices, crumbled
- One-half C. heavy whipping cream
- 4 oz. cream cheese, softened
- 4 tbsp. butter, softened
- 1 tsp. seasoned salt
- 2 C. Monterrey Jack cheese, grated and divided

Direction

1. Preheat oven to 500 degrees.
2. Cut potatoes into thin wedges and transfer to a large bowl.
3. Add 1 Tbsp. oil, and salt, to bowl. Toss to coat.
4. Separate potatoes into 2 even piles on baking sheet.
5. Bake 4 hours, turning once. Remove from oven and let cool.
6. Turn oven to broil. Combine cream, butter, and 2 tbsp. of cheese.
7. Place potatoes into 2 10-oz. or 1 6-oz. oven-save bowl.
8. Top with half of the cheese, then half of the cream mixture.
9. Repeat layers. Broil until cream cheese is bubbly and golden.
10. Top with remaining 2 tbsp. olive oil and seasoned salt.
11. Serve.

Nutrition: Energy (calories): 1192 kcal Protein: 36.96 g Fat: 72.77 g Carbohydrates: 102.32 g Calcium, Ca600 mg Magnesium, Mg154 mgPhosphorus, P730 mg Iron, Fe5.82 mg

Mouthwatering Cauliflower

Preparation time: 15 minutes

Cooking time 30 minutes

Servings: 8

Ingredients

- 2 large heads cauliflower head, stem removed and cut into 2-inch florets
- 3 tbsp. olive oil
- Salt
- ground black pepper
- One-fourth C parsley, chopped finely

Direction

1. Control the frequency of the grill to 500 degrees F and set the temperature this for 15 minutes with the lid close.
2. Add cauliflower florets, oil, salt and black pepper and toss to coat well.
3. Divide the cauliflower florets onto 2 baking sheets and spread in an even layer.
4. Place the baking sheets onto the grill and cook for about 20-30 mins, stirring once after 15 mins.
5. Transfer into a large bowl.
6. Add the parsley and toss to coat well.
7. Serve.

Nutrition: Energy (calories): 65 kcal Protein: 1.52 g Fat: 5.32 g Carbohydrates: 3.95 g Calcium, Ca26 mg Magnesium, Mg14 mg Phosphorus, P34 mg Iron, Fe0.8 mg Potassium, K244 mg

Super-Addicting Mushrooms

Preparation time: 15 minutes

Cooking time 45 minutes

Servings: 4

Ingredients

- 4 C. fresh whole baby Portobello mushrooms, cleaned
- 1 tbsp. canola oil
- 1 tsp. granulated garlic
- 1 tsp. onion powder
- Salt and freshly ground black pepper, to taste

Direction

1. Put a Traeger Grill fire to 180 degrees F and pre - heat for 15 mins with the cover closed, using charcoal.
2. Add all ingredients and mix well.
3. Place the mushrooms onto the grill and cook for about 30 mins.
4. Preheat the Grill to 400 degrees F and preheat with closed lid for 15 mins.
5. Place the mushrooms onto the grill and cook for about 15 mins.
6. Serve warm.

Nutrition: Energy (calories): 69 kcal Protein: 4.08 g Fat: 4.21 g Carbohydrates: 6.08 g Calcium, Ca7 mg Magnesium, Mg17 mg Phosphorus, P166 mg Iron, Fe0.52 mg Fiber2.8 g Sugars, total2.78 g

Veggie Lover's Burgers

Preparation time: 20 minutes

Cooking time 47 minutes

Servings: 6

Ingredients

- Three-fourth C. lentils
- 1 tbsp. ground flaxseed
- 2 tbsp. extra-virgin olive oil
- 1 onion, chopped
- 2 garlic cloves, minced
- Salt
- black pepper
- 1 C. walnuts, toasted
- Three-fourth C. breadcrumbs
- 1 tsp. ground cumin
- 1 tsp. paprika

Direction

1. Cook lentils by boiling in 2 qt. salted water for 25 minutes or till tender. Drain. Heat oil in a large nonstick skillet over medium-high heat. Add onion and cook for 5 to 7 minutes, until onion is translucent.
2. Place one-fourth cup lentils into a food processor; add 1 tbsp. flaxseed and 1 tbsp. water. Blend until smooth. Add flaxseed lentil mixture to skillet and cook for 1 minute. Add garlic, salt, and pepper; cook for 2 minutes. Mash mixture with a potato masher.
3. Combine the rest of ingredients in a food processor. Puree until the mixture forms a dough. Add one-fourth cup breadcrumb-walnut mixture to the remaining lentils in the skillet and cook for 1 to 2 minutes, until the mixture is dr.
4. Heat the smoker to 400° F. Line a baking sheet with parchment paper
5. Shape the lentil mixture into four 3-inch patties. Place patties on prepared baking sheet and bake for 45 minutes, until golden brown.
6. Put burgers on a bun with your favorite toppings.

Nutrition: Energy (calories): 157 kcal Protein: 3.95 g Fat: 11.68 g Carbohydrates: 12.07 g Calcium, Ca32 mg Magnesium, Mg39 mg Phosphorus, P93 mg Iron, Fe1.37 mg

Satisfying Veggie Casserole

Preparation time: 15 minutes

Cooking time 50 minutes

Servings: 10

Ingredients

- 5 tbsp. olive oil, divided
- 6 C. onions, sliced thinly
- 1 tbsp. fresh thyme, chopped and divided
- Salt and freshly ground black pepper, to taste
- 1 tbsp. unsalted butter
- 1 and one-fourth lb. Yukon gold potatoes, peeled and 1/8-inch thick slices
- One-half. heavy cream
- 2 and one-fourth lb. tomatoes, cut into one-fourth-inch thick slices
- One-fourth cup black olives, pitted and sliced

Direction

1. Heat 3 tablespoons of the olive oil over a medium-high flame. Cook onions, stirring occasionally until they turn translucent. Sprinkle thyme and add salt and pepper to taste. Continue cooking for 5 to 10 minutes over a medium heat. Stir occasionally.
2. Heat a grill to medium-high. Brush potatoes with the remaining olive oil and arrange in a single layer on the grill. Cook for 8 to 10 minutes, until lightly browned, turning once. Cut into half- inch thick slices.
3. Preheat oven to 375°F. Sprinkle olives on top. Pour the heavy cream over tomatoes. Cover and bake in the oven for 30 minutes or until bubbly and golden brown.
4. Enjoy!

Nutrition: Energy (calories): 158 kcal Protein: 2.74 g Fat: 9.31 g Carbohydrates: 17.97 g Calcium, Ca45 mg Magnesium, Mg29 m Phosphorus, P80 mg Iron, Fe1.48 mg Potassium, K529 mg

North American Pot Pie

Preparation time: 15 minutes

Cooking time 50 minutes

Servings: 10

Ingredients

- 2 tbsp. cornstarch
- 2 tbsp. water
- 3 C. chicken broth
- 1 C. milk
- 3 tbsp. butter
- 1 tbsp. fresh rosemary, chopped
- 1 tbsp. fresh thyme, chopped
- Salt and freshly ground black pepper, to taste
- 2 and three-fourth C. frozen chopped broccoli, thawed
- 3 C. frozen peas, thawed
- 3 C. chopped frozen carrots, thawed
- 1 frozen puff pastry sheet

Direction

1. Heat the oven to 450, and lightly grease a mug or small baking dish.
2. In a large bowl, dissolve the cornstarch with the water. Stir in the broth, milk, butter, rosemary, thyme, salt and pepper.
3. Add the vegetables and stir. Add the filling to the cooking dish.
4. Lay the puff pastry over the filling, and tuck the sides into the dish so that the pastry overlaps.
5. Bake for 50 minutes, or until the pastry is brown. Serve hot.

Nutrition: Energy (calories): 76 kcal Protein: 2.55 g Fat: 4.28 g Carbohydrates: 7.79 g Calcium, Ca64 mg Magnesium, Mg14 mg Phosphorus, P55 mg Iron, Fe0.49 mg Cholesterol13 mg

Potluck Favorite Baked Beans

Preparation time: 15 minutes

Cooking time 2-3 hours

Servings: 10

Ingredients

- 1 tbsp. butter
- One-half of red bell pepper
- One-half of medium onion, chopped
- 2 jalapeño peppers, chopped
- 2 (28-oz.) cans baked beans, rinsed and drained
- 8 oz. pineapple chunks, drained
- 1 C. BBQ sauce
- 1 C. brown sugar
- 1 tbsp. ground mustard

Direction

1. Prepare your Smoker and heat it for 450F.
2. Melt butter over medium heat and sauté the spices for about 4-5 mins.
3. Transfer the pepper mixture into a bowl.
4. Add remaining ingredients and stir to combine.
5. Transfer the mixture into a Dutch oven.
6. Place the Dutch oven onto the grill and cook for about 2-3 hours.
7. Serve hot.

Nutrition: Energy (calories): 86 kcal Protein: 0.97 g Fat: 1.48 g Carbohydrates: 18.57 g Calcium, Ca16 mg Magnesium, Mg12 mg Phosphorus, P22 mg Iron, Fe0.42 mg Fiber1.1 g

Traditional English Mac n' Cheese

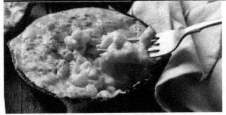

Preparation time: 15 minutes

Cooking time 30 minutes

Servings: 10

Ingredients

- 2 lb. elbow macaroni
- Three-fourth C. butter
- One-half C. flour
- 1 tsp. dry mustard
- 1 and one-half C. milk
- 2 lb. Velveeta cheese,
- Salt
- black pepper
- 1and one-half C. cheddar cheese, shredded
- 2 C. plain dry breadcrumbs
- Paprika

Direction

1. Cook macaroni for 8-10 minutes under directed time in boiling water. Reserve 1/3 C. of macaroni water. In separate sauce pan, melt butter. Stir in flour and mustard until smooth.
2. Add milk and cook over medium heat, stirring constantly, until thickened and bubbly. Stir in cheese and macaroni water. Season with salt and pepper. Add cooked macaroni to saucepan and stir to coat with sauce. Garnish with the extra cheddar cheese and dust with the bread crumbs and paprika. Place in a smoky grill in a 300-degree Fahrenheit oven for 20 minutes or until golden brown. Serve immediately.

Nutrition: Energy (calories): 951 kcal Protein: 41.91 g Fat: 35.95 g Carbohydrates: 113.49 g Calcium, Ca998 mg Magnesium, Mg77 mg Phosphorus, P1850 mg Iron, Fe2.94 mg

Amazing Irish Soda Bread

Preparation time: 15 minutes

Cooking time 1 hour and 15 minutes

Servings: 10

Ingredients

- 4 C. flour
- 1 C. raisins
- One-half C. sugar
- 1 tbsp. caraway seeds
- 2 tsp. baking powder
- 1 tsp. baking soda
- Three-fourth tsp. salt
- 1 and one-fourth C. buttermilk
- 1 C. sour cream
- 2 eggs

Direction

1. Preheat the Traeger grill to 375 degrees F. Mix the dry ingredients together in a large bowl. Be sure to measure and combine well.
2. Add the sour cream, eggs, and buttermilk into the dry ingredients. Mix until all of the ingredients are wet. Remove the dough from the bowl and form it into a rectangular loaf.
3. Bake for 60 minutes at 375 F. After 45 minutes, remove the baking sheet from the oven and spread what remaining dough there is into a wider loaf. Return to the oven for the last 15 minutes or so.
4. Allow to cool for 30 minutes. Serve.

Nutrition: Energy (calories): 286 kcal Protein: 9.71 g Fat: 6.25 Carbohydrates: 47.1 g Calcium, Ca132 mg Magnesium, Mg21 mg Phosphorus, P197 mg Iron, Fe3.08 mg Potassium, K288 mg;

Native Southern Cornbread

Preparation time: 15 minutes

Cooking time 30 minutes

Servings: 8

Ingredients

- 2 tbsp. butter
- 1 and one-half C. all-purpose flour
- 1 and one-half C. yellow cornmeal
- 2 tbsp. sugar
- 3 tsp. baking powder
- Three-fourth tsp. baking soda
- Three-fourth tsp. salt
- 1 C. whole milk
- 1 C. buttermilk
- 3 large eggs
- 3 tbsp. butter, melted

Direction

1. Sift together the dry ingredients. Then add the wet ingredients. Stir just until moistened, but do not overbeat.
2. Put a 3-quart cast iron skillet in the preheated oven and heat oven to 375 degrees. Pour the batter into the hot skillet and return the skillet to the oven. Bake cornbread for 25 to 30 min. until the top is golden brown. Remove cornbread from the oven and let it sit for 10 min. before serving.

Nutrition: Energy (calories): 259 kcal Protein: 6.42 g Fat: 11 g Carbohydrates: 33.67 g Calcium, Ca176 mg Magnesium, Mg18 mg Phosphorus, P246 mg Iron, Fe1.31 mg Fiber1.2 g

CONCLUSION

In conclusion, it is a fact that the Traeger pellet grill has made grilling easier and better for humanity, and Grilling, which is part of the so-called "dietetic" cooking, had been made easier through the Traeger grill. Giving us that tasty meal, we've been craving for and thus improving the quality of life. This book made you a lot of recipes that you can make at your home with your new Traeger Pellet grill. The recipes will give so much satisfaction with the tenderness and tasty BBQ.

The Traeger barbecues are electrical, and a typical 3-position function controls them. A cylindrical device transmits the pellets from the storage to the fire place, like a pellet stove. Traeger Grill smoker promotes an excellent outcome for your meat and other recipes. This smoker provides a tasty for your foods. To achieve such a real taste, you need the quality of materials and get the exact smoking. It is best if you get the maximum consistency of smoking so that you can have the best result of your meat and other recipes. Moreover, if you add more flavors to your recipes, use the best wood pellet for cooking for your food.

Many people ask me questions on why I chose Traeger pellet grill, and you might think, well, the answer is clear and true, and yes! It's right before us. Why?

It cooks with a wood fire, giving an excellent quality in taste because nothing is like it: real wood, real smoking, natural aroma. In terms of the cooking process, it has changed a lot. Experts chefs tend to have new experiments with new flavor and ingredients to create a delicious and tasty recipe.

Grilling is one of the most popular cooking processes that grant a perfect taste to your recipes. Grilling is a much healthier method than others because its benefits food, preserves flavor, and nutrients. But from the other side, a Traeger grill smoker's wood pellet grill allows you to grill your food quickly and with less effort and smoke. The advantage of having a Traeger grill smoker in your home is the versatility, helps you cook food faster, provides a monitoring scale for the temperature, and it is one of the essential parts of cooking.

It is a versatile barbecue. In fact, it can be grilled, smoked, baked, roasted, and stewed—everything you can imagine cooking with the Traeger grill smoker. You will find that this Traeger grill smoker is a flexible tool that has a good service.

As we all could testify that using the pellet grill has been made simple by Traeger: its intuitive control panel has a power button and a knob that allows you to adjust the temperature comfortably.

Finally, we need to note that through Grilling, we can always find new flavors in our dishes: with Traeger pellets, you can smoke your dishes, giving them an ever new and different flavor. Traeger Grill smoker is the answer you are looking for your taste buds. Don't waste your time and have your own smoker at home and start cooking your favorite recipes with this book.

CPSIA information can be obtained
at www.ICGtesting.com
Printed in the USA
LVHW061103080221
678123LV00026B/14